Copyright

Text copyright © 2016 Danielle Tate. All rights reserved.

Information contained within this book may not be copied, published, or otherwise shared without the author's express written consent. Please visit www.danielletate.org/contact with questions.

Scripture quotations marked AMP taken from the
Amplified® Bible,
Copyright © 2015 by The Lockman Foundation
Used by permission. (www.Lockman.org)

Scriptures taken from the Holy Bible, New International Version®, NIV®. Copyright © 1973, 1978, 1984, 2011 by Biblica, Inc.™ Used by permission of Zondervan. All rights reserved worldwide. www.zondervan.com The "NIV" and "New International Version" are trademarks registered in the United States Patent and Trademark Office by Biblica, Inc.™

Cover photo by Ally Summers

Thank You

What can I say. The love Christ had for me, even in my sin is beyond my comprehension. In some small way, my Thank You to Jesus is writing this and sharing it with you. His healing was not just for me, but for you as well. So, thank *you* for having the courage to buy or accept this book and read it.

A special thank you to my husband, Brad. Thanks for putting up with emotional baggage early on in our marriage, and not giving up. May He heal you of past hurts, as He has healed me.

In Him,

Danielle

Table of Contents

Foreword 6

Introduction 9

The Truth About Modesty 13
    What Modesty Is Not 15
    Modesty Is About Identity 18
    Modesty As A Sacrifice 25
    Modesty As A Witness 30

A Holistic Look At Purity 41
    How Purity Gets Lost 42
    Erotic Novels: Safe or Seductive? 51

My Story, My Mess 63
    Marriage – A Not So Happy Ending 67
    Behind the Pain: The Birth of One Ugly Baby 72

The Road to Restoration 79
    Repentance and Confession of Sins 80
    The Three Keys of Forgiveness 83

The Ties That Bind 97
    Soul Sisters – Unhealthy Friendships 107
    Breaking Soul Ties 111

    Breaking Vows 120

    Physical Reminders & Gifts 123

Living Victoriously 126

Identifying Roots 130

    Weeding Out Abandonment 133

    Weeding Out Other Roots 137

Conclusion 148

Resources 150

About the Author 152

Foreword

So many of us struggle with shame. Shame about what we did. Shame about what was done to us. Even shame because we did things we never believed that we would do--we're not even the person we thought we were.

And now we're hurt. We don't always understand why we can't seem to move on, but the pain won't go away.

In Restoring the Lost Petal, Danielle wants to help you end that hurt. She takes you on a journey to understand why your heart doesn't feel whole. She helps you to understand why you did things you never thought you would. But even better--she takes you to the other side to show you that this is not all there is. You can find that joy and peace again, and you can feel whole again.

On my blog, I hear from so many women who are worried that they have done something irreparable. They've lost "their purity", and now everything that they will ever have, they figure, is second best.

But our purity has nothing to do with what we do with our bodies, and everything to do with what Jesus did with His.

If you don't understand what I mean by that, don't worry. Danielle's going to fill you in, and it's the secret to true freedom! But maybe intellectually you know what I'm saying is true, yet that head knowledge doesn't silence the condemnation in your heart. It doesn't help with the fact that you still feel an irresistible pull to someone who hurt you so badly. It sounds like it's just words.

It's not. It's powerful. And that's why this book isn't just a book of words; this is a book that will help you examine yourself (even if that's messy!), and help you journal and pray through your experiences so that those moments from your past don't have to define your present, or your future, anymore.

You can move on. You can move forward. Read this book, do the exercises slowly, and you will!

But what you will move towards is different from what you were before. Yet it's not less-than. It doesn't take you backwards; it takes you forwards, through grace, through forgiveness, through healing, so that you become wiser, more mature, and more able to help others.

That's what Danielle found in her own life when she finally found peace. And that's what she wants to share with you.

I hope you'll let her--because Jesus doesn't want you stuck!

Sheila Wray Gregoire
Author of The Good Girl's Guide to Great Sex, and blogger at *ToLoveHonorandVacuum.com*

Introduction

We make a futile attempt to measure sins, one against another, to justify our behavior or make ourselves feel better. Yet, to God, all sin is sin. The understanding of this simple, yet profound truth should not haunt us or make us hide in shame. The revelation of this in our lives should make us rejoice at his mercies. We can fall to our knees in worship knowing that every sin, no matter how "big" or "small," is washed clean thanks to Christ. Each sin has a unique set of consequences, some small, some large, and those are the effects we deal with here in this life (and ultimately in eternity). But his mercies are new every day. They are new every day because every day we need mercy, every day we sin, even if "just a bit." If the God of the universe can forgive our daily trespasses, however seemingly insignificant yet all-too-frequent, then we can forgive ourselves and open the door to healing.

Restoration comes in part when we allow God to heal us, but also when we allow His healing to penetrate our lives. If a doctor had a pill to cure your ailment, it would do you no good to leave the pill on your front porch. You must bring in the medicine, accept it, and believe that it will cure you of the unwanted issue.

So it is with our Lord. He stands and knocks. With Him comes salvation, healing, and restoration.

My prayer is that these words resonate deep within you, giving you a longing to live purely and modestly. To allow the Lord to heal you of past sins that are holding you back from all the pleasures God has for you.

More so, I pray that these words open a door for conversation with your friends, daughters, nieces, and other young women in your circle, so that they can be spared the hurts and pain I, and perhaps you, have endured, or so freedom and healing can rush in like a flood and restore them, like it has me. I tell my story openly and honestly because I am no one special, just a lost little girl who was healed by the one and only true God.

Modesty and purity are more than just our clothing and our actions, though they have a great deal to do with it. Both characteristics are matters of the heart. Setting our hearts on these things will cause our outward appearance, speech, and actions to change.

It was not until well into my 28th year that I realized the significance of my actions. I carried much baggage into my marriage. Thanks to restoration, I see clearly who I am and what I'm called to do. I thank God that I have moved past these dark days of guilt and shame. No more is sex marred by the shadows of my past. I worked out my restoration hanging on to God's hand, and often crying at the foot of the cross. Your story, similar to mine or different, did not end yesterday. The past does not have to be the backdrop of your future. What you are doing now does not have to be the way you live the rest of your life. With God, all things are possible, including restoration, which will allow you to live a thriving life.

As you read on, let the Lord reveal Himself to you through these pages.

Let the written words soak in deep, Lord, and cause this precious reader to examine their heart and life, and seek healing where needed. Father, I thank you that that these words are being read by

those you destined to read them. I pray nothing leads them astray or hinders their walk in the areas of purity and modesty. I ask for your healing touch and your wisdom, Father.
In Jesus' mighty name, Amen.

Shall we?

The Truth About Modesty

Do you not know that your bodies are temples of the Holy Spirit, who is in you, whom you have received from God? You are not your own; you were bought at a price. Therefore honor God with your bodies.
~ 1 Corinthians 6:19-20

Modesty. It's a scary topic. There seem to be as many people championing the cause for ankle-length skirts and turtlenecks, as there are those rockin' low-cut tops and yoga pants at the mall. There are several reasons modesty is important to us as Christian women. Some are more familiar than others. I want to address a few of them here for you. When you think of modesty, what do you think of? Covered body parts? Closed lips about your consummated relationship? No unwholesome talk? As I've grown to understand the dynamic, intimate relationship Jesus seeks with each of us, my views on modesty have changed. I stand by what I have written in the past, but I believe a deeper, prevailing reason for modesty exists, and it comes from living in relationship with Christ and gets its roots in the very core of who we are.

Modesty at its core is much deeper than the tired pants or skirts argument. Its purpose, rooted in protecting these earthly vessels – both body *and* soul – is to keep what is sacred from the snares that can so easily entrap us.

> *Your beauty should not come from outward adornment, such as elaborate hairstyles and the wearing of gold jewelry or fine clothes. Rather, it should be that of your inner self, the unfading beauty of a gentle and quiet spirit, which is of great worth in God's sight. For this is the way the holy women of the past who put their hope in God used to adorn themselves.*
> ~ 1 Peter 3: 3-5

I do not believe this Scripture is telling us not to braid our hair, put on jewelry, or wear fancy clothing. Instead, it is telling us that what we adorn, or garnish ourselves with, is that which makes our inward beauty shine through. Our spirit, which is precious to God, should be the last thing we "fix" before we walk out the door – not our hair. When we "check" ourselves in the bathroom mirror, are we also doing a heart-check?

We want to be a pleasing aroma to the Lord not because we have to clean up, but because we want to give Him our best. We are not modest just because Pastor, or Mother, or Teacher says to do so. We are modest because our hearts are being transformed, and in that transformation, our outward actions and appearances change. It's what makes the mini-skirt wearing, club hopping, boobs popping, 20-something start covering up in the first place. Not because it's more fashionable, but because something deep down inside wants to change, needs to change.

You may be thinking you're pretty modest, or you believe you're so immodest (or have been) that you'll never be able to change. I encourage you to seek God in this area. Let him flesh out areas of pride, judgement, shame or guilt you might be carrying. Modesty is a wonderful, biblical thing, but it is quickly taken to extremes by man, and the Enemy, and used as weapon against us.

What Modesty Is Not

Modesty can be a slippery slope that quickly leads us further from God instead of closer to Him. When modesty comes before or is used in place of a true heart change, then we've bastardized a wonderful thing. Modesty cannot take the place of Christ in our lives. It doesn't save us, justify us, or make us worthy of standing in the presence of God. It won't take away our demons, it doesn't clean up our conscience any more than the old saying, "cleanliness is next to godliness." I have read far too many articles of women saying how close to God they feel when they're in a dress, or how dirty they feel wearing pants. If you have accepted Christ as your savior, accepted His invitation to live in you, change you, and redeem you, than you are one with Christ. You are not closer to God by what you wear, you are closer to God because of the One who died in your place.

Modesty is not about sexuality. Here again, I have heard and read many misguided teachings that, purposely or not, gauge modesty around the sexual feelings of men and women. I do believe today's over-sexed and over exposed culture is a challenge for many men, which I'll discuss a few pages from now, but in no way is modesty meant to snuff the fire of our sexual being. Men and women were created to experience sexual and sensual feelings. We will feel them regardless of how we dress. Modesty was never meant to be a tool to crush sexual desire and dampen sexual appetite.

We are made in the image of God, and God's creation is good. We ought not to be ashamed of our beauty or our bodies. We should not shame away the very thing God fashioned with His own hand, in the name of modesty.

> *"So God created man in his own image, in the image of God he created him; male and female he created them."*
> *~ Genesis 1:27*

> *"God saw all that he had made, and it was very good. And there was evening and there was morning – the sixth day."*
> *~ Genesis 1:31*

There should be no shame in the beauty we possess, for that beauty came from God and is good. Modest dress, behavior, speech, and actions are an act of love toward our Creator and ourselves. Modesty is remembering that God also created us to glorify Him, and it speaks of the self-worth we have, because we know to whom we belong. The woven fabric of human action and reaction was designed with modesty in mind. It benefits everyone.

Modesty is not about acceptance. If your purpose in dressing modestly is to garner attention or acceptance from men, or women, you have a problem. No matter how much of you is covered or not covered, if your heart is seeking only to please women by looking like them or rack up glances from the boys, your issue will not change with your outfit.

Modesty *is* about identity. Only when we come to understand who we truly are, can we clearly see a case for modesty that transcends culture and denominational doctrine, both created by man.

Modesty Is About Identity

Modesty does not birth identity, identity gives birth to modesty. Self-justification through modest behavior is a false savior. There is only One who saved us and only One in whom we find our identity. We must understand the value of our relationship with Christ because in Him is where we live, move and have our being. Before we can discuss modesty we must discuss who we are and whose we are.

We are three-part beings: body, soul, and spirit. This earth suit, our body, is a temporal vessel we use to interact with the natural world. God fashioned and formed our earth suit as the place for our spirit to reside. Our bodies are beautifully made. They aren't meant to bring us shame nor are they meant to be the currency used to buy acceptance and fake love. Once saved, God's spirit joins with our spirit and we become a temple. What we see is the residence of God Himself.

Paul explains to the people of Athens that,

"The God who created the world and everything in it, since He is Lord of heaven and earth, does not dwell in temples made with hands; nor is He served by human hands, as though He needed anything, because it is He who gives to all [people] life and breath and all things. And He made from one man every nation of mankind to live on the face of the earth, having determined their appointed times and the boundaries of their lands and territories. This was so that they would seek God, if perhaps they might grasp for Him and

find Him, though He is not far from each one of us. For in Him we live and move and exist [that is, in Him we actually have our being], as even some of your own poets have said, 'For we also are His children.'
~ Acts 17:24-28 (AMP)

Do you not know and understand that you [the church] are the temple of God, and that the Spirit of God dwells [permanently] in you [collectively and individually]? If anyone destroys the temple of God [corrupting it with false doctrine], God will destroy the destroyer; for the temple of God is holy (sacred), and that is what you are.
~ 1 Corinthians 3:16,17 (AMP)

Paul tells the people that God does not dwell in temples made with hands. Later, he tells the church in Corinth where God dwells. This is significant to us as we begin to understand our identity. Keep in mind, this body is not our identity. It is only the vehicle we use to travel in this earthly realm. The spirit lives in the body and the spirit is where our identity comes from. Before I understood what Paul was saying, I thought that the church (the four walls and ceiling) was where God lived. But 1 Peter 2:5 reminds us that the house of God is a spiritual one:

You [believers], like living stones, are [a]being built up into a spiritual house for a holy and dedicated priesthood, to offer spiritual sacrifices [that are] acceptable and pleasing to God through Jesus Christ.
1 Peter 2:5 (AMP)

It's hard to look in the mirror and see past the physical features and flaws. May I suggest you don't even try. You can't see the things of the spirit with your natural eye and when you look into the mirror all you'll see is the flesh staring back at you. Instead, turn to scripture and to the relationship you have with Christ to understand who you are.

Know who you are:

You are loved by God. His love overshadows all that we've done, are doing and will do. He doesn't love us because we qualify to be loved, He loves us simply because He created us and we are meant to be His. As if it needs proving, He laid down His very life, through Jesus Christ's death on the cross. (Romans 5:8; John 17: 23; John 15:13, Eph 3:17-19)

You are precious because you were purchased at a high price. His death on the cross was for you. A person's value is not in what the world thinks of them but in the price paid on the cross for them. (1 Corn 6:20, Revelation 5:9, Romans 5:8)

You have been declared innocent. Once you repent, you are innocent. The blood of Jesus cleanses you. (Galatians 2:16)

Our conscience is clean. You are allowed to have a clean conscience. Satan wants nothing more than to stop you from having a clean conscience by reminding you of your sins. But Truth says, "*my scars have paid the price.*" You are no longer a sinner, you're a saint!

Your sin is no longer part of you. We no longer claim our sins. Jesus took them from us. (Romans 3:22: Romans 3:25, Romans 5:17)

We are new in Christ! We are not just sinners saved by God's grace. We are new! We are saints! This is our new identity found only through what Christ did on the cross for us because he loved us more than life itself. (2 Corn 5:27; Eph 4:24, John 1 12-13; Galatians 2:20)

We are now in a position of authority. We are seated with Christ at the right hand of God. This is a place and a position of authority. We're saints with power and authority over our past, our present and our future. Satan's lies and agenda of confusion are powerless if we get this. (Eph 2:6; Mark 16: 15-18; Revelation 5:9-10)

Once you understand the truth of your identity, your mindset will begin to change. You will find that you want to think, act, speak, and dress modestly because you are a masterpiece, crafted by the Creator. You are a daughter of the King and what else should a daughter clothe herself in but the most beautiful of adornments? The root is not pride or arrogance, but of knowing who you are representing. You are His and you are confident in that identity.

If you were preparing to meet a king you would probably put on your best outfit, maybe even buy a new one. You'd watch your manners, you'd study the proper way to eat a meal in the palace, and you would carefully measure every word that rolled off your tongue. You may never find yourself in the presence of earthly royalty, but the reality is that you are indeed in the presence of heavenly royalty every day. You can walk in His presence every day. He expects your spiritual attire to be of royal stature, and heart to be of noble character. What you chose to put on your earth suit represents the presence of the King in your life. Your King does not demand the finest money can buy. He doesn't expect you to show up only upon invitation in only the best dress. Instead, He expects you to listen to His voice and to heed the direction He gives to you. In this way, modesty is your outward declaration that you are a daughter of the King of kings.

We are not to be clothed in culture but in character. Godly character stems from the understanding that we are not just thrown together lumps of cells but a masterpiece, crafted by the hand of God himself. We can be fashionable and modest. We can be relevant and modest. We can even have fun and be modest. It's not about rebelling against pop culture, but about living our lives as the royalty we are through Christ Jesus. This revelation allows us to look properly at other effects of modesty in the world.

Modesty As A Sacrifice

When I first read Shaunti Feldhaun's book *For Women Only*. I was stunned. It was the first time I had ever heard the idea of a "visual Roladex," as she puts it. The fact that a man, who I did not know, could revisit an image of me at any moment was shocking. I thought it was fun to have guys notice me at the club and want to dance with me. What I didn't realize, or think of as fun, was that these guys could recall images of me later in life. I did not want my body to be in some man's mental digital picture frame.

A large majority of men are visual. Their brains store "photographs" of things they see. These photographs are like a photo carousel or a digital picture frame. Spin the carousel or turn on the picture frame, and any image will pop up. They cannot control what image will appear. When they see a beautiful woman, their brain takes a snapshot and stores it like an image on the memory card in your phone. At any given moment, that image can flash back to them as clear and vivid as the moment they first saw her. It does not matter if the man is a pastor, teacher, father, husband, co-worker, classmate, or jerk from the mall (or the nightclub). God's great design made men visual.

You may think you deserve to wear those skinny jeans, or that you look cute in the 2-piece bikini, and to your girlfriends, no doubt, you do look cute. However, to the men and boys around you, cute and deserving do not stop the memory card from filling up. If the men who see you this way are godly men they may resist the temptation to look too long. They may know you'll come back into their mind and they pray against those thoughts. If the men who see you are not Christian men well, let's say what they are thinking won't be flattering or cute. Your identity as a daughter of the King should drive you to want only the best to be thought and seen of you. You are responsible for your representation of the King, the men around you are responsible for how they view you.

Let me illustrate it this way: At a 4-way intersection, all four cars must stop and yield to each other. If they yielded all day, no one would get anywhere. If they all went at once, there would be an accident. The drivers do not assume the other motorists are going to stop. It is each motorists' responsibility to do their part to stop. You can't say *"Well, they will stop so I don't have to"* or *"It's their responsibility to stop."* All four motorists have an individual responsibility to stop, pay attention to the others, and proceed with caution.

Modesty is your sacrifice at the 4-way stop sign. You are at one stop sign - across from you are the hundreds of men who see you throughout life. To your left is the World with her passenger, Pop Culture. To your right are the Media and their van full of advertisers, marketers, and sales analysts. The Media is hell-bent on running the modesty intersection; in fact, they do not even know it exists. The World and Pop Culture don't think it's cool to stop - no one else is, so why should they?

But you stop, and then you proceed with caution. Some would say, *"Well, those men are just perverts. They need to get a life and stop thinking about girls in bathing suits like that."* I am not suggesting that men are off the hook for their thoughts. They must stop, too, and yield to the traffic of the world and let it pass by. The Bible clearly says we are to take captive every thought. A man can choose not think on the images that pop into his head, but that does not leave us women off the hook, either. We are on a dangerous slope when we think that we play no part, or have no responsibility. They are responsible for the thoughts and images they dwell on and we are responsible to carry ourselves with dignity as daughters of the King.

If you had a girlfriend who was trying to stay away from chocolate, would you offer her chocolate every time you were around her, or would you be sensitive to her desire to not eat chocolate and put the dish of M & M's away when she came to visit? I am suggesting that you put your M & M's away. Men have enough M & M's to avoid just going to the grocery store.

Even Christian men stumble and fall, and have issues from their past that can easily be a trap. A man's visual senses are to draw him closer to his wife, so that when temptations come his way, he can recall the wife of his youth and be satisfied by *her*, not some gal from the mall (or the church pew behind him). Men hold the responsibility of taking every thought captive, but let us not be like the adulteress of the Proverbs, leading men astray.

The facts are these:

- *Pleasing image (no matter the age, content, or context) is stored.*
- *Digital picture frame runs constantly (it must have Energizer batteries).*
- *Images appear at random (with no control.)*

That is the process. It's God's process for all the men you know. We cannot fault the entire male gender for the way they were created. Do not judge the man who struggles with impure thoughts - even if he knows the value of modesty, immodest images are around every corner. Pray for him, do not find fault and judge.

When you wear something less than modest, you are presenting yourself for a photo session. You will not see the proofs, you will not edit the images. Only the photographer will see them, and he may see them often. *This is not a photo session you want to take part in.*

Ask the Lord to give you a heart for the men around you. Most were crafted at God's hand to be visual. Let that help you understand your role in modesty as a sacrifice. You can only control *your* actions and words. If you are strikingly gorgeous in the eyes of man, you can be in a potato sack and still be in his digital frame. At that point, it is up to him. We cannot walk around in sacks for fear that we might make another stumble, modesty as a sacrifice means we give up the right to say and do as we please to display Christ instead. We dress knowing that we are part of the equation. We are not to blame and we aren't the bearer of soul responsibility. The enemy twists this and some church sects have bought the lie that women are responsible for men's lust and sexual misgivings. Modesty as a sacrifice means understanding our role, not taking on more responsibility that we're given.

Modesty As A Witness

Being modest in dress, actions, speech, and thought makes us a living example to the world around us. Society's perception is that we cannot have fun and be free unless we are uninhibited and do as we please. But if we, without stiff-necked religion, allow the Lord to show us how to be modest and yet still laugh, joke, have fun, and enjoy true freedom, we are some of the best witnesses the world will find.

I know a beautiful family who practices modesty in all forms as part of their everyday lives. It's how they live. I've witnessed their oldest son excusing himself to put a shirt on when I showed up to buy eggs, and their daughter using simple camisoles and t-shirts to turn modern, cute dresses into cute *and* modest dresses. They have fun, they laugh, they joke, and they even tease each other, but the atmosphere in their home is made up, among other things, of modesty. There is a sweet smell about this family, and it isn't high-dollar perfume. They understand their identity and it's evident to the people around them.

You should leave behind the sweet smell of Jesus Christ when you leave the room. Skirt or pants, v-neck or turtleneck – it doesn't matter. After all, the Holy Spirit dwelling in us is what gave us the desire to be modest in the first place.

If our hearts are right and pure before the Lord, no matter what stage of the modesty journey we are on, we cannot allow judgment to enter. We should not judge our sisters in Christ who are on similar but different journeys, nor can we judge those lovely ladies who know nothing of what modesty is about. Judgment does nothing but prove that we think we are as holy and mighty as God. I don't know about you, but I could live in a skirt, never tell a crude joke, and always wear long sleeves, and I will still never measure up to the mighty and holy King of Kings.

The Bible tells us we are made new, and it tells us we must continually renew our minds. As we grow in our walk with Jesus, our understanding of our renewal grows and our minds begin to shift perspective. As this happens, our attitude toward how we think, act, talk, and dress will begin to change. Outward modesty is a reflection of the heart change that is happening, and continues to grow, within us. Modest dress is not a badge to be worn with honor. It's to honor the One who made us in His image, and to honor the beautiful body we were given. People should leave your presence not remembering what was different about your attire, but that something was different about *you*, something refreshing, inviting, and sincere. Modesty as a witness to others is far more than a skirt or clean joke. It's a seed planted, a representation of your life, changed by Christ. One day at work, I made frequent trips to the bank, but one visit required I go to the lobby. Waiting in line, I spotted a young woman, probably my age, in a cute denim skirt with a button up sweater and a cute pair of sandals. I smiled inside and thought, "If I could coordinate an outfit like that, at least I'd look better when I wore skirts!"

The Lord arranged for her stay at the window to be long, and for my place to be at the teller next to her. While they counted my deposit, I overheard her say a few things that did not sound very loving, meek, kind, or Christian. Immediately I heard the Lord say, *"Wearing a skirt does not make you a better Christian."*
He is so right.

......For the mouth speaks what the heart is full of.
~ Matthew 12:34b

Wearing modest clothing does not make us better Christians. Moreover, it does not immediately make us modest women. It is, in my opinion, a part of the lifestyle of modesty. If our hearts are not right, are we not just like the Pharisees of Jesus' day - walking around "showing" our religiousness but never really living out our faith?

I pass no judgment on the woman at the bank. I have no idea where she'll spend eternity, or where her heart lies. Perhaps she is a beautiful Christian woman who momentarily fell into the trap of gossip and judgment (haven't we all?). God put her there to *speak to me*, not for me to judge her. She was His reminder to me that He ultimately wants not only my appearance to be modest, but also my heart, mind, and mouth as well. See, if we wear a skirt only to show off how modest we are, we aren't modest at all. In the same token, we can wear pants that are loose fitting yet stylish, and be modest, because our hearts are pure before the Lord and our outward appearance is an outward expression of that heart.

This is something you must prayerfully consider for yourself with God's guidance. Whatever you choose to wear, remember that you are a silent witness for Christ with your garments. Your responsibility is to be seen as a Daughter of the Most High. You represent Him. The changes in your heart reflect in your attire. At the end of the day, *you control you.* Modesty is a choice we make in both how we dress and how we behave. Modest dress does not equal modest heart, but is a growth from it.

Reflection Time

When you walk out the door for school or work, have you ever stopped to fix your spirit before you leave? *Yes through prayer and readings*

How could you check your spirit on a regular basis like you might your hair or make up?
Check motives and that heart is right before the Lord.

What do your friends and family say about modesty?
Be demure.

How does their influence effect your thoughts and actions?

It makes me realise that if I dress provocatively for e.g it attracts the wrong attention and is not becoming for the Daughter of a King.

If you begin to dress, act and speak differently, how would your friends, family or co-workers respond?

They would be pleased

Are you prepared to defend your decision?

Yes

Ask the Lord to give you the words to speak that are firm, but spoken in Love, and ask Him to solidify this decision in your spirit and soul so you can remain firm in the midst of opposition, teasing and jest.

Have you ever encountered someone who appears modest from the outside but does not have an inner heart of modesty? What impression has that given you about how we should dress and act?

Me. It has given me the impression that the inside should match the outside.

How do you define modesty?

Acting with a pure heart and behaving like a child of a King. ie dressing demurely. Having a humble but gentle spirit.

Modesty – throughout the Bible, the words translated to modest(y) have the following meanings: gentleness, humility, meekness, humbleness of mind, innocent, pure, clean, of good behavior.

Sum up the biblical concept of modesty based on the definition above:

Gentleness of spirit, humbleness, innocent and pure and clean of heart, and noble

If you decide to change your wardrobe, what can you do to guard your heart from the spirit of pride and judgment that will try to creep in?

Faith that the right reasons for doing it are relevant.

What would "removing the speck" from our own eye look like when it comes to modesty? Would it mean we must be perfect to help others or do you think there's more to it than that?

Don't compare self to others - keep humble

How does it feel knowing that the men in your life have a visual picture frame in their heads that may include pictures of you?

Violated

Let's reexamine your life. Is there anything that would need to change in order for you to live modestly? (Think about people, places, dress, words, and actions that may need to change)

Wear modest clothing
Be gentle in spirit
Speak words of encouragement
+ no lewd talk or action

A Holistic Look At Purity

I remember the first time I heard women called by a derogatory name. It was in song lyrics that a friend was listening to. I was quite confused as to why she'd listen to music that talked so bad about the very essence of who she was. I was shocked but it soon wore off because this was the music of our generation and in my quest to be relevant among my peers, this is what I had to enjoy hearing. I shoved aside the feelings that it was wrong, and something I should have stayed clear of. That small voice inside me was Holy Spirit. I could barely hear His whisper over the voices of my generation, but He was there, quietly whispering that I was losing parts of myself I'd have a hard time regaining.

When images, words, and ideas begin to go down a dark path, innocence is being lost. Purity breaks down over time, little by little, without us realizing it. We can dress as modestly as the Amish, but if our hearts and minds have been exposed to impure and immoral messages, we have still lost some purity.

Purity – the word purity has several meanings throughout Scripture: chastity, cleanliness (the quality of), innocence, pureness, holiness, sanctification, incorruptibleness

Do not give dogs what is sacred; do not throw your pearls to pigs. If you do, they will trample them under their feet and turn and tear you to pieces.
~ Matthew 7:6

In the verse above, Jesus is speaking and telling the people not to "throw their pearls before pigs." The wild pigs in parts of Palestine were capable of vicious attacks on humans. Wild pigs will rip apart and destroy whatever they choose.

The most precious pearl you have is your purity and innocence. Purity of soul, spirit, *and* body.

How Purity Gets Lost

You have probably heard of looking for love in all the wrong places. This is a dangerous practice where we medicate our pain by looking for love through approval from others. In the same way, learning about love in all the wrong places is a dangerous pathway so many of us fall victim to.

As a teen, I grew up watching Beverly Hills: 90210 and Melrose Place. These were fictional television shows, but to teenage girls they seemed like real life stories of what love and life was all about. Dating a bad boy and hoping one day he'd love you as much as you loved him. Being "okay" after losing your virginity and breaking up. Somehow recovering from this was as easy as getting a new haircut and a cuter, more popular boyfriend. There is no shortage of television shows and movies that wrongly influence what we think love, sex, and intimacy are all about.

When we try to live out these fantasies in real life, we end up with hurt, shame, and guilt. Our purity gets lost trying to find a life that does not exist. Even if we don't do the things we see on these shows, it exposes us to fantasies that, later in life, we will still never see in reality. Over and over, we see people do things that aren't okay, and we slowly get desensitized to fantasy, as the line between fiction and non-fiction is blurred. All of this exposure leads to purity and innocence getting lost little by little before any sexual contact begins.

What is purity and why does it matter so much?

During medieval times, purity was held in very high esteem. "Purity" was sometimes checked before and after a marriage was consummated to ensure the bride was a virgin. This was taken to extremes, and I am quite sure women were unnecessarily chastised and shamed due to unreliable, and downright cruel, practices. In medieval times, this issue became an obsessive distraction. Motives may have started out as protecting purity and honor, but it got out of hand quickly. We should not take purity to this extreme. Sadly though, the pendulum has swung too far in the opposite direction for many people. We lose our sexual purity long before we have sexual intercourse with someone, and often times we don't even realize it's happened.

Purity is not taught, much less sought after, these days. Purity seems to be a passing pleasant thought that we think of in terms of babies in little booties and small children playing in fields of flowers. Children grow up, and parents mistakenly think they are protecting their children by allowing them to experience things well above their age and maturity, in an effort to make them "wise" to the world around them. After all, the world is not all sunshine and roses, and we must be wary of what lurks in the shadows.

We must be aware of the how the enemy operates, but that in no way means we must lose our purity and integrity along the way. It does not mean we should not teach our children, girls and boys, about the value and need to remain pure. Purity is not the same as naïveté.
Naïveté implies one is simple minded and unsophisticated, with lack of judgment or experience. On the other hand, purity is innocence, free of guilt, shame, and unnecessary soul ties.

> *How can a young person stay on the path of purity? By living according to your word.* ~ Psalm 119:9

In today's culture losing one's virginity, male or female, is looked at as a goal, a prize, and a choice that makes one an independent individual, in control of their lives. Unfortunately, none of that is true. Losing our purity is far from a prize, and it actually ties us to people for years, sometimes a lifetime. When we lose our purity, specifically our sexual purity, we add a "modifying addition." We create a soul tie with the person whom we have sexual relations. These soul ties follow us from one relationship to the next. It does not matter if you're 15 or 55, you will carry them with you forever if they are not dealt with.

The loss of your purity does not change when you update your Facebook relationship status, or remove all the pictures of the two of you from Instagram.

Over Purified

In some religious circles, purity is still as big a focus as in medieval times, and just as unhealthy. The clothing one wears is not the only indication of purity, nor does it keep one from being impure. Separating the boys from the girls by a seam in the middle of your legs is not going to keep boys from a second glance and girls from wondering what boys think of them. Being over purified by outward appearance is not a good indicator of your heart.

When we were in our twenties, a friend of mine recommitted her life to Christ, this time for good. She desired to please God and move as far away from the old self that was replaced with her new life. (See 2 Corinthians 5:17) One day, on a visit several months after this transformation, I found her and her darling girls had chosen to wear skirts exclusively, no pants. At the time, my relationship with Jesus was coming back into alignment, but I was a bit shocked by what I saw.

There's nothing wrong with wearing skirts or trashing your current playlist of songs for music that Jesus would listen to. In fact, as we work out our salvation and our relationship with Christ grows, we often find ourselves exploring what is right and acceptable to Him. Please don't confuse what is acceptable to Christ with what is acceptable to man. There are non-negotiables in a relationship with Christ, just like any committed relationship, but there are also personal convictions that only Jesus and you, guided by the Holy Spirit, can decide.

My friend was doing what she saw others in the church doing and what the pastor had expected of the women in the church. She had not come to the conclusion through her relationship with the Lord, only through what man was deeming holy and acceptable. This is a slippery slope. We do not need to be acceptable and pleasing to man in order to be worthy of time with the King. I fear too many religious houses place an emphasis on the outward before the inward when God is asking us to come to Him, as we are and he'll clean us up from the inside out.

Either way, too much emphasis or not enough, purity needs to be a comprehensive, holistic study in God's word, that looks at the inward and the outward, and is always, always held up to God's standard of love, sex, and intimacy.

Woman of virtue

Reflection Time

How would you define purity?

Cleaness holiness
Sanctification
Innocence
sexual purity
purity of mind + soul

What do you think it means to live a pure life?

Living according to Gods word
Avoiding unnecessary soul ties
Acting and dressing worthy of
being a royal princess of the
King. Follow guidance of HS

What do you consider the opposite of a pure life?

Debauched lewd crewd
dirty, perverse, sadid cruel

Read Psalm 119:9; what does this scripture tell us about purity?

By living according to God's word we can be pure

What areas are you throwing your pearls to pigs?

music
men
images
dress

How can you guard your heart against impurity?

Listen to music worthy of a child of God, watch and wear wholesome things

Only allow sex in marriage with a man God has brought into your life

Erotic Novels: Safe or Seductive?

The television is not the only place delivering this desensitizing and distorted view of love, sex, and intimacy. Erotic novels have infiltrated the lives of scores of women, even Christians. Often called "mommy porn," these novels take women on a fantasy journey that leaves many dissatisfied with their marriages, and leave singles and teens with a warped sense of what love should look like. Erotica novels are not new, but they are gaining steam in pop culture. As I'm writing this, 50 Shades of Grey is the newest, hottest, and most sought after book (and movie) among many women, even Christians. This book has somehow drawn the attention of millions. Over 70 million copies sold to readers in the first year, to be exact. Even professing Christian women are reading 50 Shades, and talking about how wonderful and harmless it is. After all, it is "just a book". Yet, Christian women are reading erotica novels like *50 Shades* at the same percentage as overall American women.

Despite what popular magazines tell you, erotica novels are far from harmless, and have many lasting effects. Let's take a look at what reading erotica will really do for you.

Erotica novels give you false hope

Erotica feeds a woman's deepest hopes. When you allow your mind to be filled with images and descriptions of fictional events and people, you eventually put hope in them and a "one-day" mentality forms.

"One day, I'll find a man like that." "One day, we'll make love like that." "One day, he'll talk to me like that." "One day, my body will have those feelings."

One could argue that this mentality can also come from stories like Cinderella, Sleeping Beauty, and The Little Mermaid, and would not be wrong, but on a much deeper level erotica pulls at your desire to be known in the most intimate way. The God-given desire to be known intimately by one person has been cheapened to a quick fix by a fictional character in a book.

Erotica novels make you disillusioned

Once you're filled with false hope, you will then look at your life and become disillusioned. The definition of disillusioned is *disappointed in someone or something that one discovers to be less good than one had believed.* Suddenly the man you married, or are going to marry, is no longer good enough. You resent that he hasn't said, done, or behaved like the men you read about. When you become disappointed, you start to look around, and when you start to look around, suddenly the other grass looks greener. You might not physically walk to the grass, but you may catch yourself dreaming about the grass on the other side so much that it consumes you.

If you're not married, the shock of reality may not hit you until after you are. Fantasy is wonderful when it never meets reality. The disappointment only comes when the two collide head on, and you're faced with the stark reality that Christian Grey doesn't exist, and your spouse will never, ever behave the way he does.

Erotica novels turn love into an idol

Have you ever read a book that completely consumed you, one you could not stop thinking about between readings? The characters seem to come alive on the screen of your mind, and you find yourself deeply engaged with them throughout the day. A brilliant fiction author can make his or her characters come alive in that way. Erotica authors are quite good at this. Their well-crafted pages are designed to draw you into their story, and turn love into an idol.

How can love be an idol? When it consumes you. When you think about it more than anything else. Love and sex are wonderful things to be enjoyed, but they are great in the context of your marriage. Good things can turn bad very quickly. I love this quote from Julie Slattery in her book, Pulling Back the Shades,

> "....A good thing that becomes the primary thing immediately becomes an immoral thing. Any good gift from God that is exalted above God becomes a tool of the enemy. Love, sex, and marriage are prime candidates."

Erotica novels lead you away from God

Would you consider erotica and street drugs to be in the same category? You should. Both have lasting effects on our brains. Erotica, street drugs, and sexual experiences cause the same chemical reactions in the brain, and leave us longing for more. Eventually, we begin to think of our drug of choice more and more, above anything else. When we are consumed by something other than God, we've begun to worship an idol, and we cannot worship God and an idol. If you do realize these books are not healthy, the enemy will switch gears on you. Suddenly, the harmless books you reasoned away as entertainment become a trap of shame and guilt that lead you further away from God. God hasn't moved but Satan will heap on shame and guilt until you feel unworthy to be in God's presence.

Satan loves to change the game. First, he'll tempt you with an innocent looking book that is enticing, mysterious, and intriguing. Once you've been snared by the fascination, he heaps it on, waiting for the kill. As soon as you realize what you are doing is wrong, he stabs you with shame, guilt, and condemnation. You may put the book down, but Satan will replay this broken record to you over and over again. It goes like this:

"How can you be so stupid? You know that stuff is wrong, and now what will your family think? You think God still loves you after that? Ha! No way can He forgive you for this. You might as well give up on God, because He is not going to forgive you this time."

Erotica novels make your sex life unsatisfying

The more times you experience pleasure while reading erotica, the harder it will be to experience pleasure or even be satisfied with normal, run of the mill sex in your marriage. This is because of the chemical response I mentioned above. New sexual experiences trigger the release of phenylethylamine and adrenaline. Like a drug addict, slowly you need more and more new experiences to become satisfied. The realities of a normal sex life without glitz, glamor, and a fictional "perfect" man, leave you less than satisfied.

Recovering from Erotica

If you have read erotica, or if you are reading it now, I urge you to look at what you are reading and measure it up to the Bible. As Paul said, everything is permissible but not everything is beneficial. Is erotica drawing you closer to the Lord? If you are married, does it draw you closer to your husband? Are you discussing the latest book with your friends over coffee instead of encouraging each other to work on your real-life relationships with your spouses? If you have been exposed to erotica, I recommend picking up a copy of *Pulling Back the Shades* written by Dannah Gresh and Dr. Juli Slattery, and digging into the longings of your heart and how erotica hurts those longings rather than fulfilling them.

This world is a dark and fallen place. As we look for an understanding of love, sex, and intimacy, we must be sure to look in the right places. It is not wrong to be curious about sexuality, sex, and love.

We must carefully choose where we are learning about love, so that we aren't losing sight of the beautiful thing God created, for the thrill of a physical high.

When we try to be pure and modest only because it has been pounded into our heads, we'll have no personal convictions and beliefs to stand on when snares and temptations come. We'll only have the words of others ringing in our ears, no louder than the words of those who want to pull us away. <u>We must set our minds and receive our own conviction on how the Lord wants us to practice purity and modesty, otherwise we'll flounder. It's called getting your own Jesus.</u> I can preach to you about *my* Jesus, your pastor can passionately tell you about *their* Jesus, and you can read testimonials and praise reports about everyone else's Jesus, but please *go get your own.*

You need to know Christ and not just as fire insurance but so you can have real conversations with tears, laughter, honesty, and counsel. It is in this personal relationship with Him that your heart, your soul, and eventually your wardrobe will change.

The foundation of healing and restoration that we'll discuss later in this book is Jesus. Without Him, none of it is possible. You can read about healing, you can understand how to break vows and renounce things you've done, but if Jesus Christ is not living in you, the work will be a futile effort. Don't just say the words to get the healing, ask Him to show Himself to you and seek to build a relationship with Him. There is no limit to the depth of a relationship with Christ. He is the only man who won't leave you, trap you, cheat on you, or lie to you.

If you don't have a personal relationship with Jesus, please take a moment to invite Him to be Lord of your life.

God,
I know I have messed up. I'm a sinner and I need your forgiveness. I know you are the one true God, and I know Jesus came to die for my sins so that I can not only have eternal life, but also be restored and healed while I'm here on earth. Please make this real to me, and help me build a relationship with You so that I can live out the destiny you have called me to. I want to turn from the things I have done that are not godly, and I want to live a better life. I trust you and I accept your forgiveness. In Jesus' name, Amen.

If you just accepted Christ as your savior, congratulations! This is the first step toward healing and wholeness. A thriving life awaits you as a daughter of the King. Go tell someone you know about the good news that Christ died for you and you are now reconciled with God because of Jesus. If you've been on the fence or gave you life to the Lord before but didn't really know what it mean now is your time. It is not about a ticket to Heaven. It's about living a thriving life right here, right now. It isn't about money and fame or social status but about becoming that which Christ died for you to be: a woman set apart for God's glory, healed from your past, touching others so they too can be healed.

In the coming chapter, you'll read my story of restoration. I pray God speaks to you through it and you find your way to accepting forgiveness and healing from the Father.

The technology of our time bring about more challenges, as ways to find impure and immoral things are only a tap or click away. Erotica novels are a prevalent part of our culture and so is online pornography. If you're reading or watching porn you are not alone. Thousands of Christian women have been drawn into this trap. Escaping it will require you to make changes and perhaps humble yourself by confessing to a trusted sister in Christ and being held accountable.

The addiction of pornography does not discriminate based on race, religion, age or sex. It's mission is to destroy that which God created as a sacred and special act.

Reflection Time

Why do you think women fall into the trap of erotica?

Because of exposure to the worlds view of sex through erotica porn, tv etc. + the physical effects - release of chemicals in brain as a result of exposure

What desires is erotica meeting for you?

It's not music makes the unacceptable acceptable. Dancing

Are there other forms or pornography you need to remove from your life?

TV Music

How has erotica or pornography distorted your view of love, sex and sexuality?

Its influenced me into thinking what it should be

What truths based on God's word can you believe instead of the lines of porn?

A woman of virtue
Psalm 119:9 .

My Story, My Mess

A few years before I met my high school beau, I made a pact with all of my friends that we would not have sex until we were married. It sounded like a good plan, but none of us – not one – kept the pact. You know why? **None of us were prepared to handle the emotions and feelings that accompany dating someone.** No one explained to us the importance of waiting, or what not waiting would do to us, and most of us were allowed to be alone with our boyfriends at ages when we never should have been allowed to do so.

I was one of the "good kids" who didn't skip school (much), never had detention, and always made the distinguished honor society. I had one F, on my Geometry midterm exam, and I cried. I was college-bound and did not care much for boys, until I met my one and only high school boyfriend.

We were 16 when we met. He was cute, he was nice, and my mom approved of him. We were both in Honor Society, got exceptional grades, and liked algebra. He didn't drink or do drugs, and he went to church every Sunday with his parents. We dated four months, and that pact I made with my girlfriends seemed like such a waste of time. *What exactly was I waiting for again?* Oh, marriage, that's right. Well, he and I planned to get married, we talked about it often, and I even decided I would move with him wherever he wanted to go to college and...we didn't think further than that. My thoughts centered on my desire to be a wife.

There was no drama in the loss of our virginity. No rebellious "doing it" because our parents said no. **We truly thought we were in love** and would get married one day. He even bought me a ring. We went too far, far too often. We talked about what we were doing. We discussed birth control - after all, having children at 17 was not an option for us. We were responsible so it was okay.

Until he broke up with me.

Like many high school relationships, ours ended not long after graduation, as he prepared for college in another state. With a shattered dream of being a homemaker, and a large piece of my soul missing, I was alone. I felt like part of me was ripped off, never to return. Shallowly, I thought it was him that I couldn't live without. I didn't realize that the hurt deep in my heart was a grieving of sorts that was not going to go away anytime soon.

I cannot recall any more of the details of this break up. However, I do distinctly remember wondering why I felt as though I lost the best part of me. To numb the pain, I rebelled against most of what I stood for. I remade myself into a total disaster. I lost weight, cut and dyed my hair, and started tanning. I was a hot little number, skinnier than I had ever been, with money in my pocket and a desire to show him, and anyone else, that I was worth being wanted. I loosely dated a guy from work for a few months only to find he was interested in my friend. Then I ended up living with a guy who cheated on me multiple times and was physically abusive. I was smart enough to end that one after the second time he put his hands on me. I had sex with both of these guys, and nearly every time I would feel horrible afterward.

I didn't know why, but something about me was wrong. I could literally feel the hole inside me, yet I could not put into words what was wrong. Not only was something wrong, there was also something missing. This feeling of being incomplete would not go away. I never knew before that heartache was real, physical pain one could experience. I was like a beautiful car without an engine. I could go nowhere, make no headway. I was stuck in park.

By this time, I was twenty-one. I found freedom in my new legality and ability to go into places where the cool people were. After the split with cheater/beater guy, I did more rebelling and loosely, this time *very* loosely, dated his best friend. I admit, it was done out of spite and retaliation. If he could sleep with my boss, I could sleep with his best friend. It was a time I am not proud of, but not ashamed of either. It's part of my life, and I can't undo it.

Soon, our fun times and overnights turned into booty calls. It sounds like something from someone else's life, but it's mine and I accept what it was. When one of us was lonely and needed a warm body to satisfy the deep longing we had to be needed, one would call the other. We would smoke weed and have sex. Sometimes I just needed to be numb so I didn't feel so bad about myself. In the morning, life was back to normal, at least for me: more emptiness, more loneliness, still missing pieces of myself.

After a few months of this uselessness, an old flame reappeared in my life. I cannot even describe what our relationship was because it was so bizarre. He was in the Navy, so I would see him a few days here or there. I was his state-side fling, some small piece of normalcy for him while he traveled on a large boat all over the world.

Marriage – A Not So Happy Ending

The pain I felt subsided with intimate connection, and what better way to have intimate connect then to be married? I just wanted to be a wife - then I would not feel so alone, so dirty, and so empty. I knew sex before marriage was wrong. My youth pastor talked about it, the church in general talked about it, so I knew, *I just knew*, that once I was married things would be better. Problem was this pool of people I'd surrounded myself with left no good choices for me to spend the rest of my life with. Then I met Brad.

It was a chance meeting at a friend's house. He was tall and handsome. He walked with a manly confidence that I'd not seen in any of the boys I'd known and dated. I was intrigued. However, let me back up a bit.

I was living the double life of clubbing Thursday through Saturday and going to church on Sunday. Only a week or so before we met, I had cried out to God and told Him I was done looking for someone to love me. I would be single forever or He had to throw someone in my lap. I sort of knew that drinking and clubbing were wrong, and I didn't like how I felt all the time because I drank so much. I knew that any attention I got at the clubs was superficial at best, and only served to please some random loser who wanted to rub up against me on the dance floor. I could not figure out how to get what I desperately needed, so I gave up.

The day I met Brad at my girlfriend's house, when I asked who he was, her exact words were *"Oh, that's Brad, he's a nice guy. He drinks a little too much, but he's a nice guy."* I didn't care about drinking at that point - I drank too much, too. In the moment he walked past the kitchen window, I knew there was something right about him. Our first date was August 23, 2002. He proposed to me on November 22nd of that year, and we were married on September 13, 2003. I knew after our second date that we would get married. *I just knew.*

We lived together before we were married, and even though I knew we were getting married, I could not shake this feeling of emptiness and guilt after we would have sex. "*It will pass once we're married and it's okay to have sex,*" I would tell myself. You can imagine my surprise when we had sex on our honeymoon, and I felt the same way. The emptiness had turned into guilt and shame almost overnight. While most couples are having great intimate relations on their honeymoon, I could barely bring myself to have sex with my husband because of the shame I felt afterward.

I forced myself for a few years to be with Brad because it was right and it was what I was supposed to do, but inside I was dying. I often cried after we had sex. I would hide my tears in the bathroom or go downstairs to do a load of wash while I cried. After a few years, I could not take it anymore, and I just stopped responding to his advances. Here we were, married, and I could not bear to have sex with him. The sad part was the cliché of *"it's not you, it's me"* was true. He had done nothing: it was my demons, but I didn't know it. It got so bad he thought I was cheating on him. Something needed to change - I didn't know what, I didn't know how, but I did know when: *soon*. You see, I had opened a door that let guilt and shame creep in. For 10 long years, these two companions never left my mind. I carried the ties I created with other men (boys in comparison to my husband) into my marriage. I did not bring them along because I wanted to. I did not bring them along because I somehow still fantasized about them or "wanted" them. The ties were unwanted, but they were not going away.

The approval process to get a new pharmaceutical drug approved by the FDA takes years to complete. Phases of trials take time, as research is done to see the effects of the drugs on users before a drug is put into the marketplace. Years are often needed because the adverse effects of drugs may not be discovered until much later. Once approved, many drugs are still taken off the market years later when negative effects become known. The negative effects of our sexual encounters are like new drugs under FDA scrutiny. The adverse reactions aren't seen at first, sometimes it is years down the road when we wake up and realize that an event from our past has left a path of destruction in our life. Guilt and shame take over, and we end up medicating with the very thing that hurt us to start with.

Behind the Pain: The Birth of One *Ugly* Baby

Have you ever seen a newborn baby? I mean a *real* newborn. Not a Hollywood baby as portrayed on television, but a real, minute-old baby covered in who-knows-what, with pasty eyes and mucous and a cone-shaped head? To Mom and Dad, this baby is the most beautiful creature ever born. To the rest of us, well, we politely say how cute he is but, really, he's not much to look at just yet.

My pain was a symptom of a much deeper issue. The roots of my past were springing up as weeds and devouring the beautiful bloom of the marriage bed. My sins had finally given birth to death. When we give in to sexual temptation, we will inevitably end up giving birth to an ugly baby. We think it's fun, popular, and it makes us feel good. Then, when we step back and look at the picture, it is one *ugly* baby whose name is Sin and Death.

The death that comes as the result of sin is not always self-inflicted. The sins of others can still cause death in our lives. No matter if past sexual experiences were willful or forced, the roots of those issues can run deep, but are often hard to spot at first. Sometimes we even see them as beautiful because we are looking through the eyes of pain. The course of chaos that begins with sexual sin is like the ripple effect of a rock thrown in a pond. The innocent leaf floating on the water sometimes gets swallowed up by the ripple when it did not intend to be affected by the rock. Sin's ripple effect reaches out through life and time, affecting others and us in the present moment and the future.

Don't misread what I wrote, *sex is not a sin*. Sex is biblical, sex is pure, and sex is holy. The church does no good by making sex out to be the bad guy. It is partaking in sex outside the marriage relationship that creates sin. It's sort of like vanilla extract. Think of the bottle of vanilla extract in the kitchen spice cabinet. Have you ever tasted vanilla alone, right out of the bottle? It smells so wonderful, velvety, smooth, and inviting. Surely, it will taste good. Do you remember your mom telling you that it did not taste as good as it smelled? But you didn't believe her. I know I didn't - I wanted to know for myself what vanilla tasted like. So you taste it, as I did, and...whoa! Nothing like you expected. It's enough to make you not like vanilla.

When you add the vanilla to sugar and cream, agitate it and expose it to the cold, you end up with ice cream. It's a far cry from the horrible vanilla straight out of the bottle. When you add sex to a healthy marriage, filled with God's blessing, the result is a beautiful, holy thing – a far cry from the sex we see pushed in pop culture. Sex outside marriage is tempting, it seems like it would be a wonderful thing. Then you do it and – whoa! Nothing like you expected. It's enough to make you not like sex ever again. Unfortunately though, the *"whoa"* sometimes does not come for days, months, or years, but I assure you, it will come. If you are reading this book because you have tasted the vanilla, then you may already know "*the whoa.*" If you don't, keep reading and you might discover that down deep the "whoa" is there. Either way, there is healing.

The temptation to have sex outside marriage is a real struggle for many people. You must understand that temptation is not a sin. We can be tempted to do and say many things every day, but only when we dwell on those thoughts, entertain ideas, and act out on those mental images, we enter into sin.

When tempted, no one should say, "God is tempting me."
For God cannot be tempted by evil, nor does he tempt anyone; but each one is tempted when, by his own evil desire, he is dragged away and enticed.
Then, after desire has conceived, it gives birth to sin and sin,
when it is full-grown gives birth to death.
~ James 1:13-15 (emphasis mine)

Satan plants a seed and watches it grow in the recesses of the human mind, as roots dig deep into the soul, and branches spread out of the mouth and hands.

Reflection Time

Do you struggle with tempting thoughts and recurring mental images about sex?

Yes

What sexual temptations have you given into or been a part of?

Lots Multiple liaisons with men Furries

Can you recall where you were and who was with you?

Yes

2 Corinthians 10:5(AMP) tells us this: *"We are destroying sophisticated arguments and every exalted and proud thing that sets itself up against the [true] knowledge of God, and we are taking every thought and purpose captive to the obedience of Christ,"*

How can you begin to take every thought captive?
By testing it against Gods word + rebuking it or dismissing it

What can you do when tempting thoughts about sexual acts (past or future) come your way?
confess repent + renounce and give to Jesus

In what ways has the past affected how you think about love, sex, and your self-image?
It's distorted it. and made me feel cheap

When old familiar thoughts comes to you, what truths can you hold on to instead?

That I am the righteousness of Christ + that his blood washes me clean.

The Road to Restoration

I often hear people say healing comes only from the miraculous intervention of God, and there is nothing for us to do in the healing process. Healing is not a hands-off experience. I believe we play a very crucial role in our healing. God does do a miraculous work in us, but the process requires much of us. Things like forgiveness, a changed lifestyle, and new thinking require us to work out our healing day by day, hour by hour, in the choices we must make – that is the price we pay for our free gift. As you begin to heal and allow God to transform your life, you must participate in several things:

- Repentance
- Forgiveness
- Breaking soul ties and vows
- Removing sentimental items
- Changing your lifestyle

The next several sections will look more closely at these key areas and help you work out your healing. Believe that God will meet you where you are, and believe that He can heal you. Your free will allows you to move forward in forgiveness and healing by making individual choices that aid in the process. Some of these areas may seem challenging to you, and you may want to skip them. I encourage you to press through even the hardest parts. Restoration and healing were paid in full by Jesus over 2000 years ago on the cross. They are a free gift, but the personal cost for walking in restoration is huge. It requires your time, your faith, and your willingness to be open to Christ's restoration process. Next, we'll look at some of the things you must consider as Christ leads you to restoring your lost petals.

Repentance and Confession of Sins

If we confess our sins, he is faithful and just and will forgive us our sins and purify us from all unrighteousness. ~ 1 John 1:9

There is such power in verbal confession. Telling what was done to you, or admitting what you did brings light into the darkness. The death grip of emotions begins to loosen when you shed light on the secrets of your past. There is no condemnation in Christ - we must admit what has happened, and when necessary we must repent.

Find an older, godly woman you can trust, and ask her if she will collaborate with you as you walk through healing. You may find support with:

- Your mom – *this is preferable if you are a teen and you have a relationship that will support such a conversation.*
- Your female pastor
- Your pastor's wife
- A church elder
- An aunt or great aunt
- A youth leader, camp counselor
- A church counselor at your congregation or a sister church in your area.
- An older sister – *here again, be sure the relationship will support this and that she can be trusted to keep what is said between you and she, and not take it to others (except your mom, if necessary).*

Verbally speaking out issues to the right person is the key that unlocks the door to healing in all forms: spiritual, emotional, relational, and physical. Darkness cannot hide in the light. That means when we confess sins or acts done to us, the darkness of Satan's guilt and shame has no place to hide. The heavy weights you are carrying around will lighten as you confess them to someone who is mature in Christ and able to guide you in the steps of freedom that follow in this book.

If there is no one you can trust, you can reach out to me and I will pray with you as your healing journey begins. You can find out how to contact me by visiting me at DanielleTate.org. Whomever you go to should be someone you are confident would not judge or add further condemnation. If no Earthly person fits for you, confess to God, aloud.

The Three Keys of Forgiveness

Forgiveness does not change the past, but it does enlarge the future.
~Paul Boese

After my grandfather died in 1996, a root of bitterness and unforgiveness began to grow in my heart. I watered it daily by entertaining thoughts of how wrong some of my family members were with their actions, or lack thereof, before Pappy died. This unforgiveness inside me clouded my judgement, influenced my emotions, and played a part in many choices I would make. Unforgiveness is a bitter pill that we keep taking. It leads to physical and emotional health problems. We were not designed to harbor unforgiveness. Our sins are forgiven because we run to the foot of the cross and surrender them to the One who died so that we could be whole. When we hold on to those sins and harbor unforgiveness, we are not following God's word. Forgiveness is key to restoration and moving forward into victory. Because sexual impurity usually involves others, forgiveness is three-fold.

Partnered with repentance is the acceptance of forgiveness. Many times in my own life, I have repented of something, yet still held myself in prison over this issue. We need to see that sin is sin, but we also need to see that forgiveness is real. Once we repent, we are forgiven, Christ steps in, and we are made white as snow. We also relinquish the right to beat ourselves up over past failures and sins at that point, too. When you are forgiven, *you are forgiven*.

Key # 1: Accepting God's Forgiveness

In him we have redemption through his blood, in accordance with the riches of God's grace... ~ Ephesians 1:7

The idea that God could forgive me for me for my sins, all of them, even my deepest, darkest misgivings, was difficult for me to accept. I felt the load I was destined to carry was a heavy one because of my choices. Daily I would relive the guilt and shame of my sins. This was my life-sentence after a guilty judgement. I could not see how I'd ever be free from my past when my past was who I was. After all, choices have consequences.

Our choices do bring about consequences, but the never-ending love of our Father reaches through those consequences. Once we have confessed our sins to God we are forgiven, and then Jesus stands between us, covering the sins with His blood. No longer are we guilty, because we have been forgiven and freed. It is as if the jail cell was unlocked because the price was paid. Your best friend served detention for you so you are free to go!

Many people find it difficult to believe that *their* sins have been forgiven and that *they* are free. The power of confessing your sins to God is that they are no longer in the dark. They are no longer grabbing at your ankles trying to keep you bound. If you are having a hard time remembering that you are forgiven once you ask, speak aloud. When thoughts come to shout, "forgiveness isn't free", or "you're still guilty and those sins are too big", shout back at the devil, "I am forgiven by the blood of Jesus!"

*If we [freely] admit that we have
sinned and confess our sins, He is faithful and just
[true to His own nature and promises], and will
forgive our sins and cleanse us continually from all
unrighteousness [our wrongdoing, everything not
in conformity with His will and purpose]*
~ 1 John 1:9 AMP

Do you acknowledge what Christ has done for you?
Yes.
_____
_____
_____
_____

When you are ready, pray this prayer not just with your mind but your heart as well. The first step in the process of restoration is to accept the forgivingness God offers as a free gift, and rest in the arms of your Father. He loves you. Your sins or the sins committed against you are not too big for Him. Close the door to those thoughts, let your past be His story and allow grace to cover you.

"Heavenly Father, you know my heart and my desire to restore my purity. I ask you now for

forgiveness from all of my past sexual sin, no matter how long ago it happened. I ask you to cleanse me with the blood of Jesus, make my sins white as snow. And now Father, I accept the forgiveness you have given me through the blood of Jesus. Please close the door to sexual sin in my life. Let it be a memory I use only as a testimony to your grace and forgiveness. I allow forgiveness to wash over me right now in this moment, and I receive your grace."

Do you accept His forgiveness?

Yes.

What does Christ's forgiveness look like to you?

Cleansing & impurity + wrongdoing
A fresh start - clean slate

Key #2: Forgive yourself

When I was walking through the healing process, I realized even once I accepted God's forgiveness I was still stuck under the heavy weight of self-judgment. I knew in my head and my heart that God had forgiven me, but I could not shake this feeling of condemnation. I quickly realized I had sentenced myself to a guilty verdict. The price was paid, the door was open, yet I remained in prison thanks to my own judgements.

The second step in forgiveness is forgiving yourself. Your flesh is weak and so easily falls for the moment, doing what feels, looks, and sounds good. Your mind, will, and emotions take you places your spirit knows it should not go. When you realize this, the enemy is quick to change up his game and start condemning you for the very things he enticed you to do in the first place. You cannot fall into the trap of self-unforgiveness and regret.

Regret is an act of your soul. Your mind reasons that what you did was wrong, and you wish you had not done such a thing. Regret and remorse are not the same as sorrow. Godly sorrow – realizing what you have done was sinful and that you need forgiveness – will lead to repentance. A repentant heart is a heart that can be healed. Perhaps you were abused and feel you could have done more to stop what happened to you. Forgiving yourself for what you could have and should have done is an important step. You are not at fault for what happened to you. Don't harbor unforgiveness for not getting out of a situation fast enough, for not saying no, for going back repeatedly for more vanilla.

The reasons do not matter, what matters is that His blood has washed you clean and He forgives you. **If Christ has set you free, you are free indeed**!

You are not the sum of your sins, and keeping yourself in grip of guilt only serves to further Satan's desire to keep you in bondage - away from the freedom and restoration found in Christ.

Do you regret what you've done or what you did not do?

Yes

When you think about the things you have done, how do you feel about yourself?

Guilty ashamed dirty unclean impure, self loathing

How do your thoughts compare to what God's word says about our past?

God says I'm forgiven set free

If you were a victim, do you understand that you are not to blame? How can you forgive yourself for that which you could not control?

I feel like it's all my fault.

What would your self image look like if you forgave yourself?

Happy + joyous. demure modest and pure.

If you have accepted Christ's forgiveness for your sins, you are free of them. Now, you must receive that truth. You must forgive yourself. Holding on to unforgiveness of yourself will keep you in bondage. When you're ready, release yourself with the power prayer.

"Father God, I stand before you now and declare that I have forgiven myself for my past sexual sins. I will not beat myself up any longer. I acknowledge what I did was wrong, and I have repented. I am

forgiven in Your eyes, and I now speak forgiveness over myself. I will no longer allow the enemy to use my past sins as a tool of condemnation. I stand blameless before You and I release my soul from self-condemnation."

Key #3: Forgiveness of Others

Resentment is like taking poison and hoping the other person dies.
~St. Augustine

The hatred you're carrying is a live coal in your heart –
far more damaging to yourself than to them.
~Lawana Blackwell

One thing remember clearly with my abusive boyfriend was that, usually on a daily basis, I told him I hated him. It started out funny. He would do something stupid or tease me, and I'd say I hated him. Eventually though, after he cheated on me, spent money we didn't have, and did absolutely nothing around the house, I did start to hate him. I said it often, and I meant it. The seething emotions inside me spewed out often. I could find no love, empathy or compassion for this person anymore. Even after we went our separate ways, my soul still hated him with burning passion. It truly felt like a live coal in my heart and the damage it was causing was very real.

Hatred and unforgiveness cause bitterness. Your time spent in anger and hate will only fester inside you. It won't hurt the other person. It doesn't make them pay for what they did. It makes *you* pay for what they did. Once married, I quickly I learned that you couldn't love your spouse with your whole heart if you are harboring emotions of hatred toward someone else. I have seen this in my life and the lives of others. You cannot go in opposite directions at the same time. When we harbor unforgiveness or hatred toward others, we cannot move forward. Those negative emotions will consume us. Until you forgive and release those in your past, you will not be able to fully love and accept those in your present and future. I know someone who harbors such hatred toward their ex that it effects their current relationship. They are unable to fully open themselves up to being loved, and to giving the fullest measure of love they have. The heart cannot hate and love at the same time. You cannot expend emotion and spiritual energy hating someone and then fully love someone else. Forgiving and releasing the people in your past will allow you to fully love your husband or future spouse.

Forgiveness is not easy. It might not come right away. Part of having an open heart is allowing God to give you the strength to forgive them, no matter how many, no matter how bad. If He can forgive them for what they did to you, His daughter, His princess, His bride, then surely He can give you the strength to forgive them, too. Forgive them by name and, if you can, by fault. I cannot explain in words the healing that comes when you release them into God's hands and stop harboring unforgiveness or hatred.

Unforgiveness manifests itself in physical symptoms like anger, rage, anxiety, and even certain illnesses. There is a spiritual link to many physical problems we experience, and many are related to unforgiveness. I won't go into more details here, since that's outside the scope of this book. I encourage you to do your own research on the spiritual/physical illness connection.

You may not "feel" forgiveness toward the people who have hurt you. It is natural to want to hang on to hate, resentment, and bitterness. Forgiveness is a choice, not a feeling. It is about releasing those who hurt you into the hands of God. They may never ask for their own forgiveness, they may never realize the impact they had on your life, but that is not your concern. You can only acknowledge this for yourself. They will have to come to their own realization with Christ. When I began to walk in forgiveness toward those who had hurt me, it was a daily choice to fight the feelings of hatred I'd grown accustomed to. Daily I gave these concerns to God and eventually my soul lined up with what my spirit knew was right in the eyes of the Lord.

Who do you need to forgive and why?

Andrew	Simon
Kian	Andrew
Clinton	Stuart
Richard Aston	Paul
Bizzo	Chris
Paul	People in pub
Tom	David JC 2000
Paul C.	MPs
Amanda	Phillip

How would forgiving someone change your thought life and attitude?

It would allow me to be free to love

"Jesus, I come to you now with a heart ready to forgive those who have wronged me or led me astray. I ask that as I speak their names and the experiences with them that you would cover them with your blood. My mind may not be ready to fully forgive, but I know that speaking out forgiveness is the first step toward realizing freedom from my past. I choose to do this in my spirit even though my mind, will, and emotions may not line up at this time."

I forgive _____ for _____. I release them to you and I declare today that I will no longer hold them accountable for my healing. Lord, forgive them and help me to forgive them now. Line up my soul with the forgiveness I am giving now so that I may walk in peace."

The Ties That Bind

When tempted, no one should say, "God is tempting me." For God cannot be tempted by evil, nor does he tempt anyone; but each person is tempted when they are dragged away by their own evil desire and enticed.
Then, after desire has conceived, it gives birth to sin;
and sin, when it is full-grown, gives birth to death.
~ James 1:13-15

Looking back at this verse in James, what is it that makes us die a little inside after temptations lead to sin? The answer is found in the bond created between two human beings who have intimate or close relationship. Friends, soul sisters, sexual partners, and vows between friends create a spiritual bond that many refer to as a soul tie.

I have watched a distant friend struggle for 2 years after breaking up with her boyfriend. Every day seems to serve only as a reminder of the relationship that is no more. Songs, phrases, sunrises, sunsets, and smells all pull her back into a pit of depression, anxiety, and inner turmoil. It has been two years and the end does not seem to come. None of this started when her Facebook status changed to single. It started way before that, back in the beginning of the relationship. As with so many of us, we don't even realize that we're forming a bond that won't easily be broken. It starts with our temptations.

When you give in to the temptation, the longing and desire for more gets stronger and stronger. The void you feel gets bigger and bigger. So, to fill the big hole, you go deeper and deeper into sin to get your fix. Flirting is not enough, kissing doesn't quite cut it, groping was good, but after a while, it's not satisfying. Finally, you have sex, and you feel like you are there, you've satisfied the desire of your heart - but only for a little while. So where is the next fix coming from?

Sort of sounds like an addiction, doesn't it? *That's because it is.*

I love how God lines it all up. Not only can we reference His word, but also we can look to the science of it all and see how soul ties work. Each of us has the Deep Limbic System created in us by God. The DLS is a set of brain structures that lies deep within your brain. It stores odor, music, symbols, and memory. You can sum this up by saying your emotional life lives in the deep limbic system. Each time you have a stimulating, pleasant experience, the deep limbic system is washed with chemicals, particularly dopamine. These positive experiences could be the smell of your boyfriend's cologne, the song you danced to at Homecoming, or the memory of the candlelight dinner where he asked you to marry him. The romantic experiences of holding hands, flirting, sexting, or phone sex all cause the deep limbic system to be washed in dopamine.

Dopamine is the "craving" chemical. It's what makes an addict need more drugs, and it's the chemical that makes you feel good. The thing about our bodies is that it doesn't matter if the "good feeling" comes from an experience with crystal meth, exercise, or porn - dopamine is released each time you experience the positive. When you experience something as pleasurable as intimate talk, touch, or sex with someone, you are creating a soul tie to them through the deep chemical bond being created in your brain. Even if it's just a friend with benefits, a long-lasting bond is being created.

When I was casually having sex with a friend, it eventually turned into a heart desire for more. After a few months, it was not enough. I wanted more from him. I wanted a relationship with meaning, something he was unwilling to give. I found myself very much connected to him in a no-strings-attached relationship. Every time the door shut at the bottom of the apartment steps, I left with a little less of myself and a little more of him, deep in my soul. We were connecting just the way God designed us to connect, with a deep, lasting attachment. Just because we were outside God's will did not stop God's physical design from working as it is created. God creates us to become intimately connected to one person of the opposite sex. It makes the bond we have with the person we are intimate with become *yada*, knowing and being known intimately, deeply. Just because we go outside his designed plan of the one-flesh relationship with one other person does not mean the chemical and spiritual bonds aren't formed.

The Hebrew word *yada* is translated in scripture as know/knew. It is an intimate knowledge of something. In Genesis 4:1, we read that *Adam knew [yada] Eve, and she conceived and bore a son Cain.* Later in Genesis, verse 17, Cain knew his wife and she conceived. When you read the scriptures where the word yada is translated to a form of "know" in English, it's clear that this knowing is not a causal connection like knowing the neighbor, your coworkers, or the kid next to you in Spanish class.

Yada is far more than physical. In modern English, it is a deep understanding and discernment. We see this explained in Proverbs 1:23: *Turn you at my reproof: behold, I will pour out my spirit unto you, I will make known my words unto you.* This isn't about reciting scripture or head knowledge, but rather knowing the Word of the Lord internally, spirit to spirit.

We can have yada understanding with several people in our life, like our children, perhaps a close friend. But only the relationship of marriage is meant to be physical, emotional, and spiritual. God knows a marriage relationship isn't going to be all sunshine and roses, so He made a way that man and woman can be tied together intimately, which will get them through the hard times. They are glued together at a much deep level.

When acts that were designed for growing and strengthening deep, intimate knowing of another person are used to fulfill desires of the flesh, the truth of God's word and his physical design of the human body don't change. No matter how much we tell ourselves *"it doesn't matter,"* we cannot change the way God created our brains. So we create the deep bonds with all the guys we have relationships with, and then wonder why it hurts so hard when they break up with us, or cheat on us, or we realize they are not the one we're supposed to spend the rest of our lives with. When we misuse what God created, we end up feeling pain and hurt. This is why we feel "broken hearted" when we break up. We truly hurt, not just in our heads or our emotions, but that physical pain is a reminder of the bond that was created with another individual. It would be like pulling apart your fingers after they've been glued together. It is going to hurt. The pain is real. The world tells us to do what feels good, say yes, live without limits, and be free. This way of thinking is not God's plan. When we truly understand that a sexually intimate relationship was designed for a specific reason, we see that what feels good (and let's be honest, sexual touch and sex feel good) has a place, but that place is not with your high school boyfriend, your co-worker, or anyone else, until that person becomes your spouse.

If you have been abused or raped, this physical contact still creates a bond that must be dealt with. Even under the worst of conditions, with trauma and pain, a connection, a soul tie can be made. Not because it was a willful act on your part, but because someone willfully chose to violate the most sacred of physical acts for their own pleasure. God's principles, His design, still works the way He intended it to. The Bible does not use the words "soul tie." However, here is a clear example of how our unwise decisions and the ungodly acts of others can create soul ties.

Now Dinah, the daughter Leah had borne to Jacob, went out to visit the women of the land. When Shechem son of Hamor the Hivite, the ruler of that area, saw her, he took her and raped her. His heart was drawn to Dinah daughter of Jacob; he loved the young woman and spoke tenderly to her. And Shechem said to his father Hamor, "Get me this girl as my wife."

~ Genesis 34:1-4

Dinah did an unwise thing by going out to "see the women of the land." In the time and culture Dinah lived in, being unsupervised in the city was a recipe for disaster. A young woman alone was exposed to the promiscuity that was rampant in that area. She would have known this, but like most teens, she still wanted to do what she wanted to do, despite consequences.

When I gave into the feelings and longing to just be wanted and needed, I ended up creating soul ties with guys I knew I'd never spend the rest of my life with. I gave each one of them a piece of me. I did not understand this going into these relationships, but I could feel the very real pain when the relationships ended.

In Dinah's story, she was raped. Though she made an unwise choice, and by going to the city alone she was raped, it was not her fault. The Bible does not say she "had sex with" it says "raped." It was an unwilling, forced act. Nonetheless, in verse three, we see a soul tie created. The soul tie was not her "love" for Shechem, but his "love" for her. The ungodly sexual sin Shechem committed created a soul tie of sexual desire to Dinah. The word translated "to love" in this verse is *ahab*, which means "to have affection for (sexual or otherwise); to be loved like, lover."

To me, this speaks of the power of a soul tie. Our soul (mind, will, emotions) can form these bonds so quickly, that even in the worst of situations, no matter if we're male or female, we can subject ourselves or even be subjected to the bondage of a soul tie.

You might be thinking that this is good - he raped her, but then he loved her and wanted to marry her. Not so. This is backward from God's plan. God does not want us to have sex with someone and *then* love them and want to spend our lives with them. This muddies the water with our emotions and feelings. When we are clouded by sexual connection, we cannot see clearly if the one we desire is the one we are supposed to spend our lives with. God wants us to choose a life-partner based not on sexual feelings, but on Truth and His will. Then, deep bonds are formed from this marriage relationship, so that, like a beautiful flower, we can bloom full and alive the way He intended.

An acquaintance of mine posted on Facebook, *"I swear, living in this 'hookup generation' will be the death of me."* If only she knew how right she was. Every time you give yourself away, you are losing a petal off your precious flower. After a while, we realize that our flower looks more like a stick because along the road of life, we have left petals behind. We cannot put these petals back on the flower. The bloom is off the rose, literally and figuratively.

God doesn't tell us to wait until marriage because He doesn't want us to have fun, or wants us to be made fun of by our peers. He knew what He was doing when He said:

> *That is why a man leaves his father and mother and is united to his wife, and they become one flesh.*
> ~ Genesis 2:24

I heard it best from a sister in Christ: "*Leave, Cleave, Weave.*" We weave together with our spouse through these intimate experiences. This is another example of a soul tie. We are not supposed to weave together with every other cute guy that catches our attention.

If your sexual experience has been one of force/rape or molestation, there are still soul ties created. Please know that these ties are of no willful doing of your own. Like Dinah, you are not to blame for what happened to you. However, also like Dinah, you have been bound by soul ties that still need to be broken. I encourage you to continue reading and break off the soul ties created from this awful experience. While you are not at fault, the reality of breaking soul ties is just as important in your healing journey.

Since soul ties can form without sexual contact, you need confess these attachments as well, in order to be healed and move on. If you are emotionally clinging to a guy who never knew you loved him, or who is dating or married, you must break this. When every song on the radio, every whiff of men's cologne, makes your heart sink a bit lower, you're attached in an unhealthy way.

Soul Sisters – Unhealthy Friendships

When I was in my early twenties, I had a friend who drug me into all kinds of crazy, unhealthy, and unsafe situations. I experienced things being with her that I never thought people actually did. I remember going home at night and wondering why I felt so bad when she was the one doing such crazy stuff. I was normally the designated driver and the one to pull her away when things were a little too crazy, and yet I felt like I was just as guilty as she was.

Experiencing these things by her side, even as a spectator, created a tie with her. It may seem strange, but you can create unhealthy soul ties with your girlfriends. If you have had an unhealthy relationship with one of your girlfriends, that can be broken too. An unhealthy relationship could be one where you have gotten into trouble with her, done wrong, sinful things, or the relationship was hurtful or one-sided. Friendship is an important part of our lives, but these relationships must be healthy and bound in Christ, not in ungodly experiences.

1 Samuel 18:1 speaks of a soul tie between friends:

After David had finished talking with Saul, Jonathan became one in spirit with David, and he loved him as himself.

You may be wondering if your friendships have gone too far. Unhealthy friendships are not hard to spot from a distance, but when you're one of the friends, it may be tricky. Often, unhealthy friendships bring out the worst in us. If your friends are not empowering and encouraging you in positive, God-honoring ways, the relationship is unhealthy. Friends should not be encouraging you to do sinful, dangerous, or spiritually damaging things.

Our friends are going to let us down, and there will be times when we disagree with them, but in large majority, our friends should be trustworthy, honest, and reliable. Most of us have friends who are casual acquaintances with whom we would not share our deepest secrets and feeling. But those we do choose to share intimate details with should be people we can trust. If those friends are constantly breaking your trust, the friendship is one-sided and unhealthy.

In life, there will be people we know and even enjoy being around, who have not reached the same level of physical, emotional, and spiritual maturity as us. You do not need to be an elitist, surrounding yourself only with friends who are much like you. There are people who we are meant to encourage and be a witness to. Not everyone will be your encourager, but you must be able to evaluate your friendships and know which ones needs boundaries, and which ones are safe for intimate, close, yada knowing.

Breaking Soul Ties

Unhealthy romantic relationships and friendships do not have to hold you in bondage forever. There is hope. No longer do I cry after my husband and I have sex. No more do I feel ashamed and guilty for enjoying sex with my spouse. I don't feel like there are any pieces missing, there's no hole left to fill any longer. I am restored, thanks to Jesus Christ. I've learned to identify toxic friendships, and I've set internal boundaries with those who are not able to respect my faith, privacy, and growth.

We cannot put the petals back on our own flower, but the One who created the flower can. God can restore us, make us whole, and make our past mistakes seems like only a hiccup – if we let Him. You can go from a victim of your emotions to a victor - a beautiful testimony of God's love, and a walking example of all that modesty and purity should be. Jesus' death on the cross covers our sins, heals our wounds, gives us reason to praise

God. His resurrection gives us hope that we, too, can overcome the death that follows these past sexual experiences.

Maybe you've heard the expression "once an addict, always an addict" or "once a loser, always a loser." This is not so with God. He loves us too much to allow us to live in hurt and shame the rest of our lives. He gave us a way out through the confession of our sins, and healing through Jesus Christ. Remember, we are a new creation. This does not just apply to limited areas of our lives.

Therefore, if anyone is in Christ, the new creation has come: The old has gone, the new is here!
~ 2 Corinthians 5:17

No matter what the circumstances were that led to unhealthy relationships and soul ties, you are not stuck in the pit forever. Jesus died to remove every stain, every sin from our lives, so that we can experience freedom, restoration, and communion with God.

Here there is no Gentile or Jew, circumcised or uncircumcised, barbarian, Scythian, slave or free, but Christ is all, and is in all.
~ Colossians 3:11

Everyone has something they wish they had done differently. I'm sure Paul had moments where he regretted killing Christians in his former life, but God transformed him and used him mightily. He can transform and use you, too, if you allow Him to heal you, and surrender the shame, guilt, and condemnation to Him. Breaking free from these chains of your past will require some effort. Once the chemical bond is formed, it can be broken only by Christ, through confession and prayer.

Flee from sexual immorality. All other sins a person commits outside the body, but whoever sins sexually, sins against their own body.
~ 1 Corinthians 6:18

We are told to flee from sexual immorality. Why would Paul use such strong language to describe our reaction to sexual sins? The transliteration of the Greek word for flee is pheugó (yoo'-go). It the above context it means to shun or avoid something abhorrent. Sexual sins are abhorrent and ugly, and they lead to death. Paul is reminding the church in Corinth that sexual sins, unlike other sins, are committed against the very person who commits them. I believe Paul points this out because He was impressing upon a city with much sexual sin, that these sins were taking the very creation of God, the body, and using it to indulge in sinful, flesh-gratifying activities.

Paul uses the world porneia in this writing, which refers to a broad range of sin, not just sexual intercourse. Again, he understood and was impressing upon the people that sexual sins are great and wide. His teaching doesn't mean sexual sin is worse than other sin, it means the effects are unique when compared to that of other sins. He goes on to remind the church that our bodies are indeed the temple of the Holy Spirit.

I read a story about a woman who was jailed after admitting that she repeatedly used meth while pregnant. She was taken into custody to protect the life inside from her. The law allowing this process is set up to protect the unborn child from mental and physical harm that would result from the mother's abuse of drugs. Like that unborn child, our spirit and God's rests inside this mortal body. Our Earth suit, as my friend calls it, is only a shell we wear for a short time. The damage done to our spirit is great when our flesh and our soul follow sinful pleasures. The Holy Spirit is called holy for a reason. It is God living inside us. Just as many of us are appalled at the idea of doing drugs while pregnant, we should also be appalled at the idea of sinning against the very dwelling place of God.

One of the greatest war waging against humanity is the lie that sex is harmless and merely designed for pleasure.

Reflection Time

Think about your past or current relationships. What is the deep down real reason you were or are in the relationship? To fill a void, fell needed or wanted, be "complete"?

Lonely, Validation to feel needed desired and wanted

Have you experienced that sensation that what you have isn't enough, and you need more, like a craving for a drug?

Yes

Can you identify the ties you have created? If not, that's okay - we'll explore this more in the next chapter.

Yes

What lies do you believe about your experience?

That if I cut them out of my life they are gone. I have also justified my behavior thinking "I'll be ok"

What does God's word say about your past? Do you believe it?

After time with your friends, do you feel better about yourself or worse?

worse

Do your friends encourage and support positive changes in your life, or do they tease and make fun of your desire to become a better person?

No

In the verse above, why do you think Paul specifically points out sexual sin?

Because of the effects on the people involved including damage to spirit

When you are ready to break unhealthy soul ties, you can begin with this prayer.

Heavenly Father,
I renounce all ungodly spiritual and soul ties with any sexual abusers, with [name of person] who I have had physical sexual contact with, with pornography and with anyone I've had a romantic relationship. Father, I repent for having sexual relationships of any kind before marriage. I ask Your forgiveness for every time I have engaged in this ungodly behavior. I know it is not your will for my life. In the name of Jesus, I break off every spiritually dangerous connection created between my soul, and that of those sexual partners. I declare my sins covered by the blood of Jesus Christ. I declare the blood of Christ is a wall separating me from these people. I release these sexual partners, witnesses, and any others that were part of this behavior to you, and I declare myself free from their ways and behavior. I do not take any consequence for their sins. I am free from them. In Jesus' name, Amen.

Breaking Vows

"I'll never leave you." "I will always love you." "You're my soul mate."

Scripture tells us that our words have the power of life or death. What we speak has eternal meaning. No matter what area of life it is, we should not be speaking carelessly about anything. And when we make vows, like the above examples, we are not simply expressing how much we love someone; we are speaking a vow or commitment to someone. The words spoken are eternal.

Often we make vows and do not realize the consequences they will have. Some we think are good, like the examples above, and some we say in an attempt to preserve ourselves from future hurts. *"I'll never get close to anyone again." "No man will hurt me like that again."* These vows leads to destruction.

You must speak, aloud, a renouncing declaration to break these commitments to whomever they were made. No one can recall all the exact words they said to someone, but you can break off any word commitments you made by renouncing any sinful word commitments in Jesus' name.

Reflection Time

We often make vows casually without realizing the consequences. Do you make vows and or speak vows over others?

Yes.

Ask the Lord to help you recall any vows you made in ungodly relationships, and write them down here:

Soul sister Donna.
I will always love you Paul/Tom.
Christian Shruf!
I will treat men the way they have treated me.
Never trust a man.

Once you have recalled theses vows, it is time to break them off.

"I renounce the vows I have made in ungodly relationships. I cut them off in the name of Jesus. I release those who made the vows with me and that I made those vows to. I cut off any spiritual ties those vows created, and I declare myself unattached and free from these chains in Jesus' name. Amen."

Physical Reminders & Gifts

I had a random bowl in my kitchen cabinet for the longest time. It was a big soup bowl, perfect for a huge dish of ice cream, cereal, or, of course, soup. Every time I'd reach for it, I'd end up passing it by and grabbing a bowl from the set my husband got us for our first Christmas together. Occasionally, this bowl would make an appearance on the table when we had get-togethers, or when someone forgot to run the dishwasher. One day, after I'd been searching my heart asking God to reveal anything I was still holding on to, He reminded me of that bowl.

My ex-boyfriend's mom had gotten me a set of two bowls and two plates when we lived together. I have no idea how one random bowl remained, but it did. I never felt right about using it, but never realized why. I just assumed the pattern did not match our décor, the bowl was too big for everyday use, or that it just wasn't my style. But my spirit knew the bowl was a symbol of not only a sinful, but an abusive relationship. The bowl went to the Salvation Army the next day, as did a few things I found in my attic after I was prompted to review the contents of old boxes and bags we had stored.

Hanging on to gifts and tokens will only keep the pain of the relationships you've had alive. Many also believe there can be a spiritual attachment to these items that affect your spiritual well-being.

When I split with my abusive boyfriend, before I even knew what a soul tie was, I could not stand the sight of his things or things we got together in our home. I gave him back his things and most of what we bought together was sold, donated, or trashed. You may miss the things you get rid of at first. Donating and selling usable items that have sentimental value is not easy, however the release that will come with freeing yourself is far more valuable than the physical possessions that can be replaced.

Lovely
Gngryenelncy

Reflection Time

Make a list of the things you can think of now that you need to remove from your home.

Lovely perfume
Engagement ring
Dignity ring ?

Are there items you feel you cannot part with? What is holding you back? What is your connection to these items?

Do you have social media reminders popping up all the time? It's okay to unfriend and unfollow. Make a list of the people and pages you need to let go of here, and start today.

Living Victoriously

As you come full circle, back to a place of purity, restored only by the Love of the Father, you may wonder what you can do practically to show outwardly the changes God has done in your heart.

First, you need to guard your heart.

Guarding Our Hearts

I think about my young niece, who dated a boy for probably 4 years, but had to break up with him. She did this because she felt he was not putting God first in his life. She had to lay him down so she could focus on what the Lord wants in her life. She did not let the pull of this world that says, "you *need* a boyfriend" drag her in, but stayed focused on her relationship with God.

I think of another young girl from our church, just seventeen, the prime age to start dating and looking for a boyfriend. However, she has made a commitment to seeking God's will for her future, so much so, that she told a boy that she could not date him when he asked. This is how we guard ourselves and remain pure - we seek God before we seek a relationship status update. It isn't a legalistic "You can't date 'til you are 20," it's a dying to self and worldly desires, and seeking God before all else. When you do, he will show you what you need to focus on, and when the timing is right, to pursue a relationship.

It is so important to think about how we can remain pure. The people we hang out with, what we watch, and what we listen to. Even seemingly harmless country music can leave us with false impressions of how a man will make us feel, or what he will say or do. Love songs are great for sparking romance in a marriage, but do not view them as the way life will be every day. It becomes hard to separate fiction from reality when we allow so much fiction into our lives on a constant basis. Fiction is all around us. It's the job of marketers and advertisers to make us buy into the fantasy world they are portraying. If we don't stay rooted and grounded in truth, it becomes so easy for fiction to seem real.

Don't misunderstand me. We don't remain pure by never dating, or sticking our heads in the sand. We remain pure by seeking God's will first, and guarding our hearts. We remain pure when we check the stuff we listen to, watch, and the people we hang out with, against God's word. When we see God as a place of refuge and safety, we can discern and judge what influences, activities, and people are right in our lives at this time.

Reflection Time

What worldly things are influencing your idea of love?

Secular music.
Comparing self with other
Mashuebher
Chara in freeds

What things might you change in your life to improve the influences affecting you?

Stop listening to secular music.
Be careful which freds to hang
out with

We cannot change with whom we work, or go to school, but we can choose with whom we hang out and give our extra time. Are your friends, acquaintances, and even family spurring you on, or are they holding you down?

Craig   Richard
Cath   Ani
Kian
Mum
Dad

Identifying Roots

As your healing journey begins, one thing you cannot overlook is identifying the roots underneath the thoughts and actions that have been your normal life in the past. These roots are what cause the mental strongholds that influence our thoughts, words, and actions. You may think your life is normal, and all of the things you have done were just willful sin. I believed that very thing through most of my healing. The truth, though, was deep roots of abandonment, and a mindset that men were never stationary, steadfast, or faithful. Like a little seed growing in warm spring soil, spiritual roots begin to take hold long before we see any growth or negative effects in our life.

Many people don't even realize roots have grown. This is because we become so accustomed to living anchored to our past by roots of abuse, abandonment, death, domestic violence, rape, molestation, or drug or alcohol abuse. Unless dealt with swiftly and holistically, events like these leave spiritual scars, and roots grow quickly. Sometimes these events are perceived dangers and over-exaggerated fears that happen in childhood. During my healing sessions with my pastor, we asked the Lord to reveal areas where the lie and fear of abandonment had crept in. One event He brought to mind caught me by surprise.

My grandparents lived on a winding country road, up on a hill. Their neighbors were close enough to be called "neighbors," but far enough away that for this elementary school girl, they seemed miles down the road. One neighbor had a dog who barked frequently, and I was told he was not a friendly dog. In fact, I was specifically told never to go up their driveway, because that dog could bite. I was not one to push the rules too much, and when Pap, Gram, or Mom spoke, I took their words at face value. Barking Dog Neighbor was off limits! Not only was I compliant in my elementary school days, I also did not speak up when I should have. So when the substitute bus driver dropped me off at the Barking Dog Neighbor's driveway, I didn't turn around and tell her this was the wrong driveway. Instead, I stood there at the bottom of their driveway, on a road I had been told was not fit for a child to walk down. I stood glancing between the driveway where I belonged, and the driveway leading to a mystery home with a dog who might kill me. What felt like hours later, my grandparents found me with tear-stained cheeks, standing at the spot where I was dropped off.

It was not really hours that had gone by, but perhaps 15 minutes or so. My grandparents were swift to call the school when the bus passed their house without dropping me off. The time that passed was what it took for the school to radio the bus driver, get the details, call my grandparents back, and for my grandparents to get in car and come for me. I was 60 yards away from where I belonged, and yet so far from home. I was all alone, scared, and helpless. Those 15 minutes were long enough for a fear of abandonment to be planted in my soul.

Through a session with my pastor, I was able to till up that seed of abandonment, pull out the roots, and see the truth that Jesus was with me even when no Earthly soul was. We must weed out the lies and "seed moments" that have warped our thinking. Abandonment was a big issue for me, and several life-events made that lie seem all the more real. Your issue might not be abandonment, but regardless what it is, you must recognize the lie and work through it.

Weeding Out Abandonment

One of the seed events in my life happened before I was even born. My father left my mom when he found out she was pregnant. Of course, I did not know this until later in life, but a root took hold and the mindset formed as I grew. My mother is a wonderful woman who worked hard taking care of and providing for me, but this root was still deep inside, and neither of us knew it even existed. The sense of abandonment can come from many things - from an actual, physical lack of presence, to emotional and spiritual abandonment. Either way, it causes hurt. Sometimes we rebel against the hurt by acting out. Growing up without my earthly father, I know what it feels like to wonder what you did wrong, why you weren't good enough, and to have the lingering lie of abandonment follow you around, even into adulthood. I stuffed these emotions down and acted as though they did not affect me. Unfortunately, they did, as the lingering sense of abandonment I carried with me into adulthood also carried into my marriage.

As daughters of the Most High, we have a spiritual Daddy, and He is a daddy far superior to any earthly father. You may not know the deep sense of physical security that comes with crawling up on your daddy's lap, or know the protective touch of your daddy's hand on your shoulder here on earth, but the love of the Father can heal you. <u>Your Heavenly Father wants to fill in the gaps left by your earthly dad</u>, as <u>He abounds in His care for you</u>. He wants to be the <u>lap on which you crawl when you have a bad day, whether you are 16 or 66</u>. He wants to delight in your successes, catch your tears when you fail, and heal your hurts. The best part is that your Daddy will not lose His temper, He won't say the wrong thing, and He will never leave you.

"I will not leave you as orphans; I will come to you." ~ John 14:18

Though my father and my mother forsake me, but the Lord will receive me.
~ Psalm 27:10

I want to encourage you to ask the Lord to show you how your earthly father's presence, or lack of, has affected your life, and what steps you need to take to find wholeness. Sometimes our fathers are physically there, but emotionally and spiritually they lack the capacity to lead as they should. This, too, can feel like abandonment. Our earthly father is also supposed to be a safe person in our lives, and the person who protects us. In order for healing to come, we must forgive those who have hurt us.

Write a letter to your earthly father. Yell, scream, cry, and be angry if you must, but let it all out. Ask the Lord to show you the emotions you have stifled, and the outlets you have chosen to take the place of your daddy. This letter is about getting your emotions out in a safe way without hurting anyone else. It does not need to be mailed or read to anyone unless the Lord tells you so, otherwise it is between you and God. If you're carrying around hurt and negative emotions, they are weighing you down.

Once you have done this, ask the Lord to help you forgive your earthly father. This process may take time, but allow Him to show you how to forgive. Start this by praying a prayer of release for your earthly father.

Heavenly Father,
I know you are the Father to the fatherless and I thank you that you have always been there and always will be. I release _____, my earthly father, to you. I forgive him for (not being in my life) or

(lacking the ability to be there emotionally and/or spiritually) and leaving me to feel abandoned by my father. Father God, search my heart and show me any areas of unforgiveness I have toward my earthly father. Heal me and take away my pain. I declare now that no matter what my relationship with my earthly father is like, I am not a fatherless child. You are my Father, my Daddy. Show me, Lord, what you would have me do to heal the wounds caused by my earthly father. Thank you for healing and restoring me. In Jesus' name, Amen.

Next, write a letter of forgiveness to him. This time you are writing FOR your dad, and ask the Lord if you are to write TO your dad also. Seek out The Father's will for this letter. It may be to tuck the letter in your Bible, or burn it, or read it to your Titus 2 mentor, or even to mail it to your earthly father, if you can reach him.

I wrote a letter of forgiveness to my father, but I did not mail it. The Lord specifically told me that this letter closed the chapter in my life, and settled forever the negative effects of my father's choice to abandon me before I was born. You may hear otherwise. If you are unsure, seek godly counsel and be sure to check your motives. Do not send a letter to stir up guilt, or condemnation, or to start drama intentionally. This will serve no good purpose.

Weeding Out Other Roots

Regardless of the cause, the roots that hold us to our past must be eliminated. This process may be difficult for you because it involves shifting the way you have thought about things for a very long time, possibly your whole life. It means changing attitude and altitude – location and logic. It means believing who you are as a child of the King, not who everyone thinks you are. I was listening to a CD of a session at Harvest Chapel, where Bill Vanderbush said this, *"You can't change your heart and God won't change your mind. But if you change your mind, God will change your heart."*

Our thinking plays such a critical role in our healing process. Once we realize how we're thinking, and how that thinking affects attitude and behavior, we realize that it all begins in the mind. We cannot change our heart - that is reserved for Holy Spirit working in us - but we can change how we think by taking our thoughts captive and clinging to truth.

Weeding out these roots of our past may mean facing some of the most painful truths in your life. Rape, incest, molestation, abandonment, and other experiences are just as painful relived, as they were when they happened. Yet, in the process of realizing these issues were pivotal moments in life, you find healing comes in the light of truth. Jesus never leaves us, nor forsakes us. Even in the darkest of places, He is waiting with an outstretched hand to begin the healing process. God is omnipresent, in both distance and time. He is still there, at the moment where your trauma, heartache, or devastation began. He's waiting with an outstretched hand to guide you into healing and wholeness.

Generational Curses are another root that can be examined. A generational curse is something that has attached itself to your family tree in a past generation through a word curse, sinful activity, or occult practices of a family member. A common example of a generational curse is alcoholism. Think about a family you know where someone struggles with alcoholism; are there others in the family who struggle too? Often times it goes back several generations.

These root causes must be dealt with in a biblical way, through the power of Jesus. As you begin your journey to restoration, it is a wise idea to seek biblical Christian counseling. You may be hesitant about counseling, but don't worry. Christian counseling that is biblically based is a wonderful aide in the healing process. Many Christians shy away from mainstream psychiatry because they feel it isn't Biblically based, but what about Christian counseling? Is counseling in all forms wrong, unbiblical, and unhealthy?

In John chapter four, Jesus gives us a clear description of the enemy and his biggest tool:

He was a murderer from the beginning, and does not stand in the truth because there is no truth in him. **Whenever he speaks a lie, he speaks from his own nature, for he is a liar and the father of lies.**
John 4:44b (emphasis mine)

Many Christians have been lied to so much they are scared of anything that seems abnormal, or uncomfortable. They try so hard not to be deceived, yet they have already been duped by the father of lies. Satan wants to keep us underfoot, when it should be the other way around. **Satan wants to keep us trapped in bitterness, anger, misery, guilt, shame, fear, and a whole host of other fruitless strongholds.** Biblical counseling can help set us free, but Satan has lied to us about that too. Jesus said:

> *"The thief comes to kill, steal and destroy; I have come that they may have life, and have it to the full."*
> ~ John 10:10

Jesus came so that we could live redeemed and restored. Counseling can help us realize, recognize, and deal with issues that have deep roots. Once we have realized and recognized, we can be set free by the blood of Jesus.

Let me dispel some lies about biblical Christian counseling:

Lie #1 - Biblical Christian Counseling is only good for stuff like worry or fear, but not "real" problems like physical pain or mental illness.

Did you know that many physical issues are symptoms of spiritual roots? Generational issues, demonic possession, roots of bitterness, self-hatred, and more can manifest as physical problems ranging from arthritis to scoliosis.

Lie #2 - Biblical Christian Counseling is just like Sunday morning service.

Counseling is not another 4-point sermon preached on a one-on-one level. It should be Holy Spirit-led therapy, in which issues are brought to light, analyzed, and prayed through with the Word of God. It should also be 100% confidential.

Lie #3 - I shouldn't have to pay for Biblical Christian Counseling - I can just talk to my pastor or my church friends.

Hopefully your Pastor is a loving, caring individual who will partner with you in prayer. However, that does not mean he or she is a trained pastoral counselor who can devote hours to study and research on counseling issues. Your friends may mean well, they may pray for you, and they may be eager to give you advice. Unfortunately, it can sometimes be hard to find friends who are unbiased. Why? B*ecause they are your friends*. They love you, they don't like to see you in pain, and more importantly, they are filtering their answers through the lens of their lives and past hurts, rather than approaching things from an unbiased, Spirit-led perspective.

Lie #4 - If the counselor doesn't have a degree in psychiatry, he or she could be dangerously wrong.

Biblical Christian Counseling should always be spirit-led - Holy Spirit-led. If your aversion to mainstream psychiatry is that it isn't Biblically based, then a pastoral counselor who is led by the Holy Spirit should make you feel at ease and at peace with taking their advice, or having them pray for you.

Lie #5 - A Christian should not need counseling. We have the Word of God, it has all the answers we need.

I saved the biggest lie for last. I could write a whole chapter on this one lie - that all we need is the Word of God with no further instruction. Let me see if I can sum it up in a few sentences.

> *"Through insolence comes nothing but strife, But wisdom is with those who receive counsel."*
> ~ Proverbs 13:10 NASB

Counsel is for the wise. To reject the need for counseling, advice, and prayer is a foolish thing. We are not meant to go it alone in this life. As the saying goes: we are not lone rangers. We see too that the Word of God is not the end all of our knowledge in the passage below:

"When the Spirit of truth comes, he will guide you into all the truth, for he will not speak on his own authority, but whatever he hears he will speak, and he will declare to you the things that are to come."
~ John 16:13 ESV

When we receive instruction, counsel, or advice from sources outside the Bible, they should always line up with the Bible. However, it is clear from John 6:13 that the Spirit speaks truth to us.

I have been to both Biblical Christian Counseling andmain stream psychiatrists. I felt more at peace, and had more breakthroughs and change as the result of Christian counseling, than in the plush office of the psychiatrists with their degrees decorating the walls.

Why?

Where the Spirit of the Lord is, there is freedom.

If you need to seek godly counsel about this, I recommend you do so. A good resource that helped me was Thom Gardner's *Healing the Wounded Heart*. It's an excellent book for overall healing. I also had the privilege of attending special sessions on Heart of the Father at our church by Bob and Kelly Parr of Freedom Question International. It was such a healing experience. The information contained in the Experiencing the Heart of the Father Manual is another awesome resource. See the resources section for more information.

Reflection Time

What are your honest thoughts about counseling?

I think it can be beneficial but not without the guiding of the Holy Spirit

What would stop you from seeking help outside your family?

Nothg

How can you overcome your fears of being open and vulnerable, so you can find restoration?

Ensure that you have a rapport/ connection with your counsellor and that they are Christian and build and trusted relationship with them.

Do you feel a lack of security and presence from your earthly father? Explain where you hurt the most.

Yes he bullies me and makes me feel small disempowered and not validated as his daughter or a human being

What does Psalm 27:10 mean to you?

Even though my mum + dad may reject me, God will receive me and not reject me.

Do you believe that you are a daughter of the King, even though your earthly father wasn't perfect?

Yes

What is your biggest challenge in seeing yourself as good enough to be His daughter?

My thought life and rebelliousness and fear of surrender/trust

Conclusion

Purity and modesty have taken on a completely new meaning to me since the Lord has healed me. Modesty is not just rules and regulations on how to dress. It is a heart change. **Purity is a precious gift, like a delicate flower.** The beautiful mystery is that, unlike petals plucked from a flower, purity *can* be restored. Once it is, we must guard it daily. We find this heart change and restoration in our relationship with Christ.

This relationship with Him is life altering, heart healing, and soul taming. It binds up the past hurts and failures, and allows us to step into the fullness of all He has called us to be. No matter our checkered past, He has a plan for us and, if we seek His will for our lives, even the most horrible of sins (as measured here on earth) cannot stop our purpose and destiny.

It is no different from any other area of life. If we overeat, He can set us free. If we drink and do drugs, He can set us free. The Cross is bigger than any sin you have experienced.

This is only the beginning for you, my dear sister. Once you have started the healing process, don't close this book and never visit the subject again. Read it often, seek God, and always – always – look both ways at the intersection. Study what Scripture says on purity and modesty. Seek for yourself His will in these areas, and never again condemn yourself for your past mistakes. After all, as they say, you can't have a message, without a mess sometimes.

Resources

Check out our **Resources** page for updated resources.

Books by Shaunti Feldhahn:

For Women Only
For Young Women Only

Books by Dr. Juli Slattery:

25 Questions You're Afraid To Ask About Love Sex and Intimacy
Pulling Back the Shades: Erotica, Intimacy, and the Longings of a Woman's Heart
Surprised by the Healer: Embracing Hope for Your Broken Story

Other Great Resources:

Healing the Wounded Heart, Thom Gardner
Experiencing the Heart of the Father, Bob & Kelly Parr

About the Author

Danielle Tate is wife to Brad, mom to Wyatt, and owner of Thrive Ministries. She is passionate about sharing biblical truth about sexual behavior, and seeing women live free from their past. She loves to write about biblical sexuality, faith, and family matters.

She enjoys time with family, camping, NASCAR, football, and coffee...*lots* of coffee. When she's not writing, she enjoys cooking traditionally prepared food, raising chickens, and planning the family's move to full time rv living. Her bucket list includes parasailing, living a short time in Alaska, and eating at Le Bernardin in New York City.

Follow Danielle:

Facebook (DanielleTateThrive)
Twitter (@TheDanielleTate)
Pinterest (TheDanielleTate)
Instagram (TheDanielleTate)
Periscope (TheDanielleTate)